A Better W

Dealing with Divorce

A guide for parents who want
to keep out of court, and save
their money and sanity

Diana Jordan LLB

for Rosie

With very best wishes

Diana x.

REVIEWS

I love the understandable and down to earth writing style of this book. It manages to cover a lot, and some of the hard truths as well.

Mrs GB, Sussex

I found this book a very easy read and liked the way it was laid out. It gave me hope in my situation where I am beginning the process of divorcing my husband after a two year separation. After my initial meeting with a solicitor I felt a mixture of hope, yet unease. I went there to discuss sorting out the financial arrangements for me and my two young children but instead spent most of the meeting talking about divorce, which I was not ready to do.

I did not move forward as it still did not feel the natural process or right direction for me and I felt frustrated, unsettled and upset about this. Then I read this book. It spoke to me and made so much sense and helped me push forward in the direction I originally wanted to go.

It actually made me cry with the realisation that there is another approach to my situation and I can do/deal with things in a different way, so thank you. As a result I have approached a mediator to try and help me/us sort out the financial matters between me and my husband. This is my utmost priority as I have two young children to look after. This book has helped me to see and navigate myself forward and put my solicitor on hold for the time being.

I found the case studies refreshing and could relate to a number of them. This has helped me rationalize things in my own head, reducing some of the constant anxiety I currently feel.

This book has made me feel and think differently and I would encourage others to read it, especially those who are unsure of the right process or order of things for them.

Mrs CE, Surrey

I started reading the extreme scenarios chapter but it was so close to home on the description of what he is like I have had to leave it until I am at home to read; otherwise I will be engrossed (and in tears) in the office.

I never knew narcissistic personality disorder existed before. I always thought I was being crazy and over sensitive or worse – he was right and I am mentally ill. Reading this and knowing that someone understands my struggle has given me the reassurance that I am not going crazy and that I need to protect my daughter above all else.

Ms ZR, Cheshire

This wonderful book really touches on things that are important from all angles. The legal stuff makes absolute sense, and the stories help to give greater understanding to the emotional fall out. After all, that is the hardest part with children to consider.

Mrs SC, Surrey

Matador
9 Priory Business Park,
Wistow Road, Kibworth Beauchamp,
Leicestershire. LE8 0RX
Tel: 0116 279 2299
Email: books@troubador.co.uk
Web: www.troubador.co.uk/matador
Twitter: @matadorbooks

ISBN: 978 1788035 767
British Library Cataloguing in Publication Data.
A catalogue record for this book is available from the British Library.

Printed and bound by CPI Group (UK) Ltd, Croydon, CR0 4YY

Matador is an imprint of Troubador Publishing Ltd

FSC
www.fsc.org

MIX
Paper from
responsible sources
FSC® C013604

CONTENTS

ABOUT THE AUTHOR

Diana Jordan worked as a family law Solicitor for many years, latterly specialising in children law as a member of the Law Society Children Panel.

In her years as a Solicitor, she witnessed the impact of our adversarial legal system on divorcing couples and their children – with the children bearing the brunt of the emotional cost.

Saddened and frustrated by the way in which the legal system let families down, Diana stopped working as a Solicitor. She now works as a Divorce Consultant which enables her to see both parties, either separately or together, something which solicitors typically won't do. Diana's aim is always to get the best outcomes for the children; she believes that the most effective way to do this is by helping parents to continue working together and avoiding the conflict, and the emotionally and financially ruinous pitfalls created by our legal system.

Unfortunately it's not always possible for separating parents to have an amicable divorce and, when one party has a solicitor, Diana works with the other if they choose not to be represented. Diana also works with parents in contact disputes when they have concerns about their children spending time with their other parent; this may be due to mental health problems, drug or alcohol dependency, or other issues such as parental alienation, which could impact their children and/or former partner.

As a member of Resolution (**www.resolution.org.uk**) Diana is committed to their code of practice which provides that members should conduct cases in a constructive and non-confrontational way. Through her continual professional development she ensures that she has a variety of tools and strategies to get people through the whole process, because different clients have different needs and challenges.

A Better Way of Dealing with Divorce is Diana's first book. Find out more about her work at **www.dealingwithdivorce.co.uk**.

FOREWORD

Obtaining a divorce in this country still frequently requires reliance on the grounds of adultery or unreasonable behaviour. Campaigns for a no-fault divorce have been rejected by politicians who feel the public will not tolerate 'divorce on demand'. Yet anyone with inside knowledge is aware that, although the divorce process is cumbersome, if it is properly followed, divorce is available for all who desire it.

The superficially adversarial process of obtaining the divorce itself is inconsistent with the drive by government to encourage divorcing couples to avoid conflict and seek agreements about their children and finances without using the courts at all. This book addresses this contradiction head on and helps provide signposts to achieve this.

The book is a survival guide for those contemplating or going through a divorce. It does not provide all the answers but does give some essential guidance not found elsewhere in a no-nonsense, easy-to-access style. A great deal of practical advice is provided on how to keep costs down. As a judge, I saw many divorcing couples painfully realising too late that far too much of their resources had been spent on legal costs arguing over issues which were never worth disputing.

There is real understanding of the emotional upheaval that the process causes and ideas on how to weather the storms. It is written by a lawyer who has insight into the needs of the divorcing client and not just for legal advice. It is something to read in full as a pathway, but also as a book of nuggets to look over when the going gets tough. Although it will be useful for anyone undertaking this painful process, its emphasis on putting children first will help a parent minimise the damage to their children, and ultimately themselves, as they navigate the choppy waters of marriage break-up.

Susannah Walker
Retired Judge of the Central Family Court, London

PREFACE

There are many books on divorce, though not an enormous number on English divorce law, considering how big a subject it is. Most of the books are written by lawyers, and largely in a language best understood by lawyers. And most of them are weighty tomes, not suited to traumatised brains. The first thing any law student learns is that law books must be up to date. Sadly many of the divorce law books available today aren't. The majority assume you're going to be using a solicitor throughout, but the reality these days is that a growing number of people can't afford to do that.

Then there's the internet, which has reams of information about divorce. Some of it's excellent, some is confusing, and some is just plain wrong. Wikivorce is a brilliant resource, although I have to confess that I often feel overwhelmed by it – and I know what I'm looking for, understand all the jargon, and know whether what I'm reading is correct or not!

That's why I decided to write a short, simple guide, to give you an overview of how it all works (as well as how it doesn't). This will enable you to research further the things that are relevant to you, without getting overwhelmed and lost in all sorts of legal technicalities that you don't actually need to know about.

I've written this book for 'Mr and Mrs Average' who can't afford all the usual legal fees and just want some help to sort things out themselves. I've made it as simple as I can, but the hard reality is that divorce is complicated and every case is different. If you don't understand something, or need some more information, please don't hesitate to ask. I'll be delighted to help you.

diana@dealingwithdivorce.co.uk

CHAPTER 1
DEALING WITH
THE DIVORCE PROCESS

The legal process in a nutshell

Information is power in separation and divorce. Unfortunately, though, our divorce law is far too complicated and most of the books about it are written by lawyers in a language that only they understand. This chapter is therefore designed to provide a rundown of divorce basics – in plain English. Armed with this information, you'll be better equipped to tackle the process with confidence.

Note that this isn't a detailed how-to book. Rather, it's designed to show you a better way to divorce, without getting embroiled in the expense and conflict of the legal system.

How divorce works

The process of getting a divorce is a fairly simple one that you can do yourself. There are (usually four) forms to be filled in by one party, and just one short form to be returned to the court by the other party. You'll find more information about filling in the divorce petition in Chapter 7.

There are two stages to a divorce: the decree nisi and decree absolute. Why we still have Latin terms for these I cannot say, but 'nisi' means 'unless'. So, the first court order (or 'decree') is only provisional. It starts the clock ticking for six weeks and one day, after which you can apply for the final order: the decree absolute.

The reason for this delay is to give time for any objection to the divorce. In almost all cases, this is a formality only; objections are as rare as hen's teeth, so unless you've been caught doing something like forging your spouse's signature, you'll be able to proceed to the decree absolute without any problems. Also, very occasionally, a couple changes their mind and decides not to divorce, and the delay allows them to back out easily.

In 99.9% of cases, no one needs to attend court; it can all be done by post. Even though the delay between decrees is only six weeks, it usually takes around three to six months to get divorced. Courts do not work fast. It can take longer if there are financial complications to resolve.

You're divorced only when your decree absolute (final order) is granted. You're then free to remarry. Legally, this is all your divorce gives you: the ability to marry again. Crucially, your divorce does not end the financial ties between you.

Tackling property, money and pensions

Many people get confused about how the divorce itself fits in with connected issues, like children and finances, and the order in which these are all tackled.

Hopefully, you and your spouse will be able to reach an agreement between yourselves on dividing your property, money and pensions, and then have a solicitor put that into an official legal document (a financial consent order) for you. You can agree all this before officially applying for a divorce – in fact, as we see later in the chapter, there are definite benefits to leaving the actual divorce petition until last.

However, if you cannot reach an agreement on financial issues, you can apply for the court to make a decision for you. This includes applying for interim maintenance if your spouse leaves you without enough to live on pending a final settlement. In such cases, you will have no choice but to apply for a divorce first; one of you will have to file the official divorce application before you can apply to the court for a financial remedy (where the court determines how to fairly distribute assets). If you need an order related to your children, you can either issue a divorce petition first, or you can apply to the court under the Children Act. In either case, before you can make an application to the court, you have to attend a Mediation Information and Assessment Meeting (MIAM) with a mediator. The idea behind this is to resolve your issues in mediation rather than in court, if at all possible.

Think of the divorce process like a tree (see Figure 1): the trunk is the divorce itself and the branches are the other proceedings. The trunk looks pretty uncomplicated, maybe even unexciting, but it's the basis of the whole structure. Without the trunk, there's nothing for the branches to hang from. The more complex the situation, the more branches there are. There can be several branches, in fact, and some of them may be complex structures in their own right, with lots of twigs and leaves.

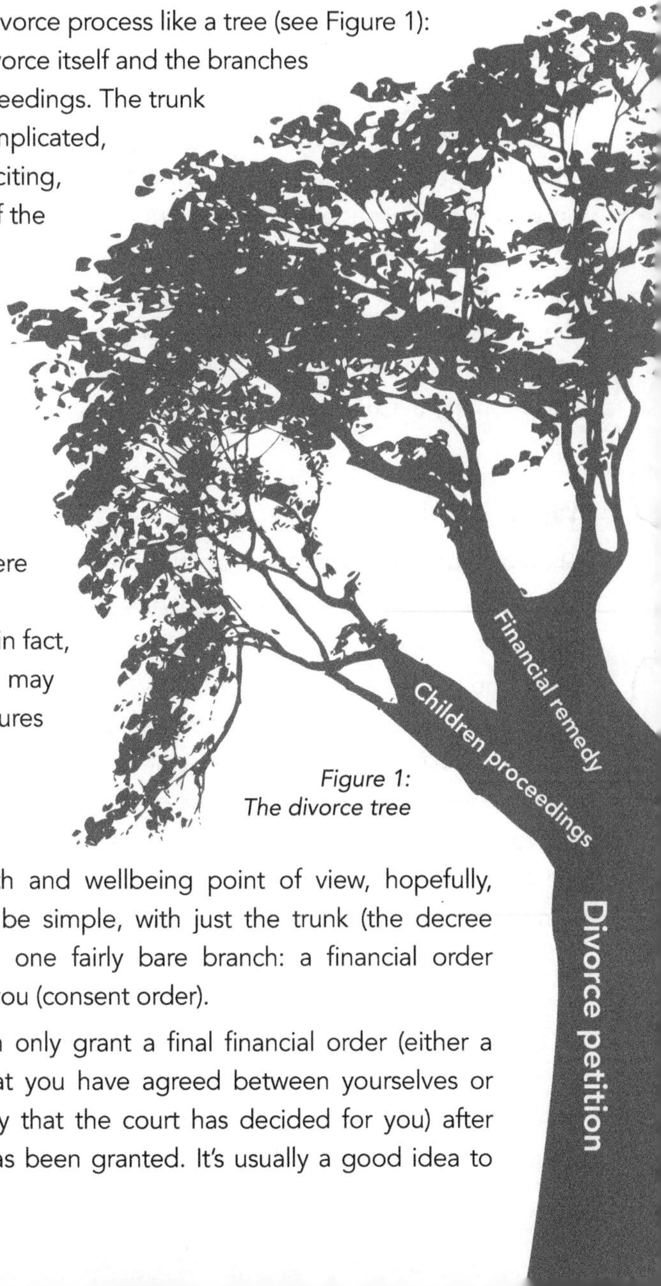

Figure 1:
The divorce tree

From a wealth and wellbeing point of view, hopefully, your divorce will be simple, with just the trunk (the decree proceedings) and one fairly bare branch: a financial order agreed between you (consent order).

The court can only grant a final financial order (either a consent order that you have agreed between yourselves or a financial remedy that the court has decided for you) after the decree nisi has been granted. It's usually a good idea to get your financial order granted by the court before applying for your decree absolute. I know it's unlikely, and not something you want to think about, but if one of you were to die after the decree absolute and before the financial order, the other would lose any widow(er)'s benefits from the state and/or any pension schemes.

Financial and property matters are separate proceedings from the divorce itself (a branch off the main trunk), and are more complicated. Unlike the divorce itself, it's unlikely you'll be able to do all of this without a solicitor. Even if you can agree on how to divide assets without getting solicitors involved, you'll still need a solicitor to draw up your final consent order, setting out what you've agreed. However, this doesn't have to mean stressful court appearances. Your solicitor can simply apply to the court for the consent order by post, and there's usually no need for anyone to go to court. You'll find more about working with solicitors in Chapter 2 and dealing with finances and property in Chapter 6.

When children are involved

The court doesn't make any orders in relation to your children unless one of you asks it to – and, even then, it will only make an order if it's better for the children than not making one.

In the normal course of events, the court asks no questions about your children and isn't involved with them at all unless you say there's a problem. You're expected to sort out their living and other arrangements between yourselves, and this can be done before officially applying for a divorce. If you think you may need some help with this, mediation is the best option. Legal aid may be available for this. There's more on living arrangements and parenting plans in Chapter 5.

If you really can't agree on what's best for your children, even with the help of mediators, one of you may have to make an application to the court. This is difficult, expensive (legal aid is not available to go to court), time-consuming, emotionally draining and, worst of all, potentially damaging for your children. Unfortunately, it's occasionally necessary, such as when a child needs to be protected from one of their parents (see Chapter 8 for help with extreme scenarios like this). In all normal circumstances, though, court should be avoided at all costs.

Taking the right steps in the right order

Knowing where (and when) to start is a key issue. If you go to a solicitor, they will usually start by making an application (issuing a petition) to the court for divorce. Before doing this, they should write to your spouse first and send them a draft petition for their comments and approval. If they don't do this, you need to ask why, as it will increase your costs if your spouse objects to the petition. Worse still, it may cause or increase animosity between you, and that is very likely to impact on your children.

I prefer to use a different approach. Wherever possible, I get my clients to delay making their application for divorce, unless they really can't bear being married a moment longer. After all, the ability to remarry is the only legal effect of divorce – and few people going through a divorce are in a hurry to remarry!

A good question to ask yourself at this point is, 'What will my divorce give me that I need right now?' If your primary need is not to be legally free to remarry, what is it? Answers I've heard typically include 'to be independent', 'to gain my freedom', 'to be shot of them', 'to sever the link', 'to get them out of my life', 'to move on with my life', 'peace', 'financial security', 'financial independence', 'justice', and 'closure'. What is it you want for yourself? Will the divorce itself give you that, or will it come only from sorting out financial and other arrangements? If you write your answers in the front of your journal (see 'Creating the ideal divorce plan' later in the chapter), it'll be easy to refer back to them when the going gets tough, or if you lose focus, and to know when you've achieved your objectives.

Figure 2 provides a visual guide to the order of typical divorce proceedings versus my recommended approach. However, it's important to note that every divorce is different and the order of applications in your particular divorce may vary in one or many ways from the order shown here. You may have more, less or no court hearings, and you may use a combination of the two models shown here.

Figure 2: The divorce process

Typical Solicitor/Court Process

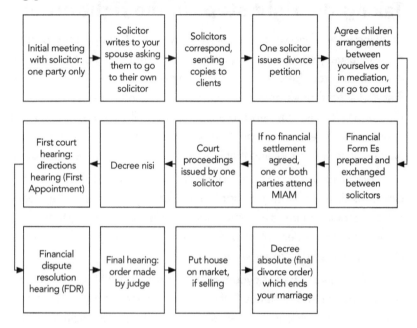

Alternative 'Dealing with Divorce' Process

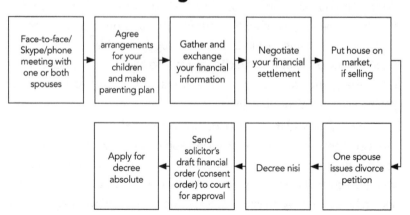

Starting with your children

The best place to start is with your children, not just because they should always come first, but because it's hard to make property and financial decisions before you've worked out where the children will be living and what they will need. See Chapter 5 for guidance on creating a parenting plan with your spouse. And remember, it's hard to think straight when you're splitting up, so it can be a good idea to get a mediator to help you make these big decisions (see 'Staying out of court' later in the chapter).

Agreeing a financial settlement

Once you've agreed where your children will live and how much time they'll spend with each parent, you can start thinking about your property and financial arrangements. You have several options for reaching an agreement:

- Over the kitchen table
- Mediation
- Collaborative law
- Solicitor negotiation
- If you still can't agree, you have two further options:
- Arbitration
- Court proceedings

I talk through these options in more detail later in the chapter.

Putting your house on the market

If your agreement or court order involves selling a property, you should only put it on the market once your financial settlement has been agreed. It doesn't work if you try to sell before you know how much each of you will get from the sale, and it can cause the breakdown of a whole chain of property transactions if you market it too soon.

If your property does have to be sold before you have an agreement in place, it's possible for your conveyancing solicitor to hold some or all of the proceeds of the sale on your behalf until you know how the money is to be divided between you.

Applying for a divorce

In my experience, there's no real benefit in applying for a divorce before you've reached agreements on the children and finances. Many solicitors prefer to crack straight on with the petition itself, but I believe it's far better to leave the actual divorce petition until as late as possible. Divorce petitions are always upsetting, so why try to tackle it while you're still ironing out the important details of your post-divorce lives? Divorce was probably the last thing on your mind when you married, so it represents the end of your combined hopes and dreams for the future. It's likely to bring up a host of other emotions, too. Plus, if your petition is based on the unreasonable behaviour of one party (still the most common type of petition), this can be difficult and upsetting for both parties. Sometimes it can lead to disputes – even an outright fight – so it's much better to have all your other agreements in place, if you can, before applying for a divorce.

Trying to resolve children and property issues is hard enough, so there's no need to make it even harder by issuing a divorce petition before it's absolutely necessary. By the time you've reached agreement on everything else, the acute pain of your breakup will be further away and it'll be easier to cope with the divorce proceedings.

However, if you're unable to reach agreement about your children and/or your financial settlement, and you need the court to decide for you, one of you will have to issue a divorce petition before you can apply for the court to make a decision.

Staying out of court

There is absolutely no need to go to court in divorce proceedings. Your forms do need to be sent there but the court can (just about!) afford the postage to send them back to you, saving you the stress of appearing in person.

Of course, you can choose to go to court to fight about your children, and/or your financial settlement, if you wish. And some people don't have a choice, say, if their spouse has issued proceedings and can't be dissuaded from pursuing them. But it's important that you know what the cost will be before you start. At the time of writing (April 2017), in the South of England, it will cost you at least £40,000 each to have a financial order decided by the court, if you are represented by lawyers throughout. In contrast, a financial consent order agreed between the two of you will typically cost between around £500 and £5,000, depending on the complexity of your particular financial circumstances.

If you want to fight over your children too, you need to add at least another £20,000 each for that, or a little less in other parts of the country. It will also take up to a couple of years to get to a final order made by a judge – precious years that you will never, ever get back. Worst of all, the only people who win in these situations are the lawyers: not you or your spouse, and certainly not your children.

If you do choose to fight it out in court, much worse than the financial and time cost (time and money that won't be spent on your children) is the emotional toll that is likely to be inflicted on the children.

Conflict between parents can be enormously damaging for children. As soon as you make any move towards a court, you're into a fight with your children's other parent. And your children will be aware of it, and affected by it, whatever their ages. You will be distracted by the proceedings for many, many months, and not fully available to your children at a time when they need you the most.

Who does go to court?

Firstly, people who want a fight.

The problem is, in my experience, they don't usually want a fight about what they're actually fighting about in court, i.e. their children or their financial settlement. What they're trying to do is settle old scores from their marriage. They each have an imagined value of the pain and suffering they experienced in the marriage and they want to get even during the divorce.

But our actual divorce proceedings don't allow for 'settling the score', as no one goes to court over the divorce itself. Well, technically speaking, if your spouse issues a divorce petition and you don't want the marriage to end, you could, in theory, ask the court to hear the case and refuse to end the marriage. But no one does this because the result is always the same: the judge will say that, if one person considers the marriage is over, they cannot be forced to stay, and the divorce will be granted. These situations are extremely rare, though.

So, if you're angry about what's happened in your marriage, you need to find another outlet for your anger. You could go on an anger management course, take up boxing, run a marathon, go for counselling or find a deserted beach and scream your head off. Do whatever you have to do, but don't do it in court! That will damage your children (and your bank account) far more than it will your ex.

Secondly, people whose spouses have a personality disorder, particularly a narcissistic personality disorder (see Chapter 8), often end up in court. My experience is that mediation is unlikely to be successful in these circumstances, as narcissists find it difficult to consider those other than themselves. This means they're usually unable to participate in the necessary give-and-take of negotiation.

Thirdly, people who refuse to give full disclosure of their income and assets are likely to be taken to court. Mediation, and any other form of negotiation, depends upon both parties voluntarily giving each other full details of all their financial assets, including property, savings, pensions and income. If you know your spouse is hiding something, you may need to go to court to get an order for them to disclose it.

The courts are getting a lot tougher now on people who try to hide things; but, if your spouse is hiding £20,000, you'll need to decide if it's worth spending that much (or more) to get an order for them to declare it. You'll probably need some good legal advice to help you make such a decision.

Fourthly, I've heard people say they want to know 'what the judge would give them'. I've found it's usually men who feel the gamble may be worthwhile for them, because they often feel they have the most to lose financially (particularly if their wives put their careers on hold to bring up the children).

There's no denying that divorce can be particularly hard on men who feel they've lost their wives, their children and their home, and they're now facing losing a large chunk of their income for the foreseeable future, and even some of their pension. It's not unheard of for men to go to two or more solicitors hoping to get more palatable advice and then decide to chance it with a court ruling.

In such situations, my advice is this: do you really want a complete stranger to make such important financial decisions that affect the future of your family? Yes, they will have a lot of information about you by the time you get to court (several lever arch files, probably), and they'll have a pretty full picture of your financial and property affairs. But they won't know what's most important to you, or that you value one thing more than another.

Your next door neighbours may have an identical house to you, but the way they live in it is probably very different; they have different needs, wants and values. That's why, after a court hearing, both parties often come away feeling disgruntled – neither has got what they really wanted. The decision has been made for them, and the decision is final.

And, when it comes to your children, no one is better placed to make decisions regarding their future and welfare than you, their parents. However well-meaning, a judge cannot know your children like you do. Therefore, I advise you to do whatever it takes to work it out between you and stay out of court. It may not be easy, but it'll be worth it. Acquiring good negotiation skills will serve you well for the rest of your life! And, as we see later in this chapter, there are plenty of options to help you and your spouse reach a successful outcome without going to court.

When children are involved, however you go about your divorce, your children should be the top priority. When trying to reach decisions, keep asking yourself this: am I really doing this for my children, or against my ex? Do I want to get even, or do I want to do what's best for my children?

What to do when your spouse has already started court proceedings

Just because court proceedings have been started, doesn't mean you'll necessarily have to go to court; it's still possible to negotiate a settlement before the first hearing, and certainly before the final one.

If you do have to go to court, make sure you're well prepared for each hearing and it won't be as bad as you fear. Be clear as to your goal(s) for that hearing, and anything you will and won't agree to in any negotiations before you actually go into court; lots of people regret things they've agreed to under pressure at the door of the court. It's also a good idea to take a friend or relative with you so you can talk over with them any proposals from your spouse. They won't be allowed to go into court with you as the hearing is private, but there's usually a lot of waiting around on your own while your barrister is talking to your spouse's barrister, and it's good to have someone with you then. For more information on working with solicitors and barristers, see Chapter 2.

Choosing your alternative to court

Resolution, a well-respected organisation of family lawyers, does a lot to promote 'alternative dispute resolution', but it's important to note that many couples don't even have a dispute – they just want some help in working out how to settle their financial affairs in a way that's fair for all the family.

For me, the day cannot come soon enough when these methods are the norm, and going to court is the alternative way of resolving disputes. With the best will in the world, there will always be some difficult cases that have to go to court, but this should really be reserved for extreme scenarios only. Let's look at the better options.

The kitchen table

When your situation is amicable and not too complicated, this is definitely the cheapest way of reaching your agreement. Just beware of agreeing to something it'll be difficult to go back on without having had any legal advice.

Lisa and Toby's story
Lisa and Toby had decided to go their separate ways. As they were still on good terms and had no children, it was all quite straightforward. They had made an agreement between themselves based on what they thought were the key factors that should be taken into consideration. However, these were rather different to those laid down by the law, which meant that Lisa had accepted far less than she would have been entitled to, and not really enough for her future needs without a much lower standard of living than she'd enjoyed during the marriage. Lisa only accepted what Toby offered her because she (wrongly) thought that's all she'd be entitled to.

Whilst of course it's right that couples should be able to come to their own agreements, the financial settlement does need to be acceptable – and fair – for both parties. Legal advice is expensive and I quite understand why people don't want to pay for it, but sometimes you do have to throw a sprat to catch a mackerel!

Mediation

Mediation is a good way to reach your financial agreement but, again, it usually needs to be accompanied by some legal advice.

I often hear people say they don't want to go to mediation because they don't want to get back together with their spouse. But the job of a mediator is quite different to that of Relate or other marriage counsellors who help couples resolve problems in their relationship and stay together.

A mediator will help you sort out the issues that result from your separation. They cannot give you advice or tell you what you should do, but they'll help you reach your own agreements. Mediators are impartial, meaning they will not take a side either way. Instead, they'll ensure your discussions are constructive and that you can both put your own points of view across.

You can either go to your local not-for-profit mediation service or to a solicitor mediator. The local service is likely to be cheaper and legal aid should be available there, if you're eligible. If there's a possibility that one or both of you may become upset or angry during the process, a mediation service is likely to be more skilled in handling these emotions. Solicitor mediators will be more knowledgeable about the law, but they have to remain neutral and cannot give either of you any legal advice.

Mediation sessions can be tough, especially if you and your spouse aren't getting on that well, but it's so much better to remain in control of the process and come to your own decisions – decisions which are acceptable to both of you. It's important to be well prepared for your meetings, and this means having a good idea of what you need to be working towards achieving for your future. You may well need legal advice before your first mediation session, and maybe further along the way too. After all, it's hard to negotiate for what you're entitled to (or something close to what you're entitled to) if you don't know what that is! Sometimes, however, there's so little to go round that the needs of the children, and their main carer, will require all the assets and 'entitlement' isn't really a consideration. In these cases, the parties are unlikely to want to spend their limited resources on legal advice.

You may be wanting a certain percentage of all the joint assets, and these can be divided up in various ways. Men can be reluctant to split their pensions, and may therefore prefer to give their wives a bigger share of the house in order to leave their pension untouched. Or, a wife may agree to a bigger share of the other assets, such as the house, so that her husband can have a clean break order (i.e. not pay her maintenance). There's no one-size-fits-all approach. The good news is, there's usually plenty of room for negotiation.

Margaret and Tom's story
Margaret and Tom reached an agreement in mediation but, when Margaret took the Memorandum of Understanding (the document that mediators produce recording the agreement) to her solicitor, she was advised that she should press for the house to be transferred to her now, rather than having to sell it when the children were grown up to give Tom a percentage then. With some

trepidation, Margaret asked the mediator to give them a further session and they managed to come to an agreement that Margaret was much happier with.

Unfortunately, not all mediation agreements have a happy ending; sometimes solicitors pull them to pieces so ferociously that the parties end up in court. This is why it's so important to be clear about what your goals are for your divorce, both financially and personally. If you've reached an agreement which meets your goals, and then your solicitor tells you you'd be entitled to more, you're not obliged to take the advice they give you. You may be obliged to sign a disclaimer to say you understand the advice you've been given and that you wish to proceed anyway against that advice, to protect the solicitor from you making a claim against them in the future. Think very carefully before doing this – ensure you have carefully considered their advice and the implications of your decisions before you sign any such disclaimer. You may also need advice, and a cash flow forecast, from a financial advisor to ensure that you'll have enough money, not just in the immediate future but possibly into your old age, too (depending on how old you are when you divorce). Whilst there's no point in going to court to fight about money if you don't need to, equally, you shouldn't settle for far less than you're entitled to because you're frightened of going to court.

Collaborative law

This is the Rolls-Royce service. If you can afford it, it's an excellent way of coming to your financial agreement. It's more expensive than mediation as you attend four-way meetings, with each of you accompanied by your own collaborative solicitor. Collaborative solicitors have done a lot of extra training, and are usually trained as mediators too. So, you both have the advantage of a solicitor there to support and advise you throughout the meetings, with the added advantage that both professionals are skilled at facilitating those types of meetings.

All of the negotiations take place during the meetings, meaning there is none of the usual solicitors' correspondence, which can easily become heated. Unfortunately, it can be expensive (but still cheaper than going to court) and, often, little is achieved at the first meeting, which is usually used to lay the groundwork. However, it's important to note that, if the collaborative process breaks down, you can't use the same solicitors if you then go to court, so there's a big incentive to reach agreement during the meetings.

As with mediation, a successful conclusion depends on both parties co-operating with the process and fully disclosing all their financial assets and income.

Solicitor negotiation

If you instruct a solicitor, they should try to negotiate a financial settlement with your spouse or their solicitor before issuing court proceedings. This will usually be done by email or letters, but it can sometimes be done by phone, particularly if the solicitors know each other.

Solicitors are usually reluctant to talk to your spouse directly if they don't have a solicitor. If you each have a solicitor, there's no reason why they can't arrange a round-table meeting with the four of you, even if they're not collaboratively trained; a lot can be achieved in such meetings, and it's much easier to have such discussions in a solicitor's office than at the door of the court. Don't be afraid to ask for one if it's not offered to you.

Arbitration

Arbitration is a relatively new, but very good, alternative to court. In arbitration, an official arbitrator reviews the situation and makes a decision that you and your spouse agree will be binding. Sometimes the arbitrator can decide just by looking at all the papers, and sometimes the parties have to attend a hearing, similar to a court hearing. A big advantage of arbitration is that you can choose your arbitrator, whereas you can never choose your judge! Arbitration also offers a lot of flexibility over the timing of hearings, and it's much quicker than waiting for a court hearing. Although you have to pay the arbitrator, it may work out cheaper than going to court, particularly if you can agree on some things with your spouse, thereby cutting down the amount that the arbitrator has to decide.

All of the above options can also be helpful if you're having trouble reaching an agreement regarding your children, although mediation is usually the best way forward for this.

Creating the ideal divorce plan

There's no escaping the fact that divorce is a life-changing process that can leave you reeling. So, when faced with the divorce process, it helps to remember the old saying on how to eat an elephant: one bite at a time. Clearly, getting a divorce is not a task that's going to be accomplished overnight. Assuming you have assets to divide and children to think about, if it's all finished in a year you'll have done extraordinarily well.

The five Ps apply to an undertaking this big:

Proper

Planning

Prevents

Poor

Performance

If you make a good plan, you can just work through it one step at a time. This will help prevent you feeling overwhelmed or getting stuck part-way through the process.

What the ideal divorce plan looks like

Your divorce plan should look something like this:

1. **Wait until your head's stopped spinning so you can think straight.**

2. **Set your goals for your divorce.** This is a journey and, if you don't set your destination in your satnav, you could be driving round in ever-decreasing circles for years. Fast forward two years and imagine your ideal answers to the following:

   • Where are you living?

   • Who with?

- How much time are your children spending with each parent?
- What is your relationship with your children like?
- What is your relationship with your ex like?
- What work are you doing?
- How much money do you have coming in?
- Which of the assets have you kept in your financial settlement?
- What problems have you had to solve to get to this point?
- What new skills have you had to acquire to get to this point?

Although it's good to think about what you really want at the end of your divorce, it's also important to be realistic: two households are going to cost more to run than one. Providing a home for your children is a priority but the aim is always to ensure that both parties are housed, if possible where the children can stay overnight. This may mean a more austere option for the parent the children are not living with.

Now, having set your divorce goals, consider whether there is anything you need immediately, i.e. anything that can't wait a year or two to be sorted out. For example, you may need more money from your spouse to pay all your bills until you can move to a smaller property, or get a new job.

3. **Choose your process**. How are you going to work all this out with your spouse? As we've already explored in this chapter, there are several options for doing this without going to court. You may use one or more of these processes for different parts of your plan.

4. **Make your parenting plan.** You need to decide where your children are going to live and how much time they'll spend with each parent before you can work out your financial settlement. A parenting plan involves a lot more than this, though, and you'll find details about how to create a parenting plan with your spouse in Chapter 5. You'll both feel relieved and more confident about the way forward once you've negotiated your parenting plan, although it may take more than one discussion to reach agreement.

5. **Gather your financial information.** This will be done with Form E if

you're using a process involving solicitors. Mediators will have their own, usually less onerous, forms to complete. Whichever process you're using, you'll need to disclose all of your assets: property, savings, pensions, cars, jewellery – anything worth more than £500. This paperwork could take a month or three to complete, especially if you have to wait for pension valuations.

6. **Negotiate your financial settlement** with your spouse via the options set out earlier in the chapter.

7. **Market any property for sale**, if that's part of your financial agreement.

8. **Instruct a solicitor to draft your financial consent order** (see Chapter 6) ready to be sent to the court once you have your decree nisi.

9. **Issue your divorce proceedings.** Your financial consent order can be sent to the court for approval as soon as you have your decree nisi and, ideally, before your decree absolute is granted.

Gathering the tools to plan your divorce

You need to treat your divorce like the big project it is, and get organised for it. It's a bit like redecorating a house. First of all, you have to decide what you want it to look and feel like when you've finished (set your goals for the future). Then you have to select your colours and furnishings (choose your process – are you going to court, or mediation?). Next is the hard graft: moving the furniture, rubbing down and preparing for painting (doing the paperwork, going to mediation, etc.). Finally, you get to do the painting and decorating (the divorce proceedings). Then, after all that work, you can sit back and enjoy a job well done.

The first thing you need to do is to go out and buy yourself an A4 ring binder and a notebook. The ring binder is for all the correspondence you'll have. Some years ago, a client told me she'd bought the most attractive one she could find in order to motivate herself to look at it, even when she really didn't want to (which was most of the time). I've recommended bright and colourful ones to clients ever since.

You'll also need a few dividers in your file, with separate sections for:

- Correspondence about your divorce
- Letters about mediation, arbitration, or whatever process you choose
- Correspondence concerning your children and parenting plan
- Letters about your house/bills, etc.
- Forms to do with your financial settlement
- Correspondence about your financial settlement
- Court documents (divorce petition, etc.)

Every divorce is different, so you'll have to make your own decision as to what sections you need in your file, and add more as necessary. The important thing is to have a file from the beginning, and not wait until you have a mountain of papers that you can't face sorting out. This is one way a divorce can get held up – and how costs rack up if the other party's solicitor keeps writing to ask for information to be provided.

It may sound silly to mention, but you should buy yourself a hole punch if you don't already have one, as even a tiny thing like not being able to punch holes in a letter can prevent someone from keeping all their paperwork safe in one place. Also, be ruthless about keeping your filing up to date; if it helps, put a reminder in your diary to do this once a week.

What if you're more of a digital fan? These days, much of the paperwork for a divorce is online anyway, so by all means keep computer records if you prefer (so long as you back them up regularly). You can make similar files and folders on your computer to keep the various documents and emails in the right places, and ensure you can easily find them again. Otherwise, simply print out the important documents and put them in your paper file.

Your notebook also needs to be attractive to look at, and preferably A5 in size so you can easily carry it with you. Your notebook is multipurpose, serving as a journal, diary, to-do list and gratitude journal (more on this later). You should update it frequently, if not daily.

Your divorce is a journey into uncharted territory and it will help you immensely if you have a place to record where you are, how far you've come, and your destination. When you're deep in the divorce process and having a bad day, it's helpful to look back at your journal and see that a bad day used to be much worse than the current one, and that you've come a long way since then.

You can either record how you're feeling on the left or right side of the pages, or write down your feelings in a separate part at the back of the book. Your journal is a safe place to vent your anger and frustration about what's happening to you; no one else needs to see what you write and you'll feel calmer around your children once you've got your feelings down on paper. At the end of each day, you can give the day a score from 0 (a very bad day) to 10 (it may be a while before you have one of those). This is a great technique, as it's clear to see when you start feeling better and things get easier.

As well as writing how you feel, challenge yourself to write five things you're grateful for each day. This will really help to foster a positive mindset, and, if you have children, it'll help you stay as upbeat as possible around them. Your gratitude list doesn't have to include big things – they can be as simple as someone smiling at you, or making you a cup of tea. At first, you may find it really hard to find your five things, but, the harder it is, the more you'll start looking for things earlier in the day. I promise you this will help you to feel better. And, on a really bad day, reading through your previous gratitude lists is sure to bring a smile to your face.

Use the rest of the notebook to make lists of things to do for the divorce, decisions to be made and conversations to be had. Record the discussions you've had and advice you've received as soon as you can, as upset or stressed brains are prone to forget. Also note any thoughts you have as you're going about your day. (You can also read this book with a highlighter pen in your hand, creating highlighted sections to revisit at various points in your divorce. You may have been taught not to mark or damage books but this is a workbook, not a sacred text!)

If you have children, it's a good idea to stick pictures of your children on the front of both your file and your notebook. They will serve as constant reminders to put your children first in all your decisions and conversations about your divorce. (But make sure you keep the file and notebook out of sight of your children, who'll be tempted to peek if they see their photo on the front.)

One of the first things to write in your notebook is your list of goals for your future, similar to your list of divorce goals created in your divorce plan. Give yourself space to go into real detail on how you want the future to look, and what you need to do to make this happen. For example, when thinking about where you'll live and how the children will divide their time between their parents, consider whether the kids will need to change schools, and whether you'll need to organise any additional childcare. Will there need to be any changes to your working arrangements? What sort of social life would you like, and how will you build it? How can you look after yourself well, both mentally and physically, through this very difficult time? Who can support you? How do you want your relationship with your ex to work? What will your divorce give you?

Cut pictures out of magazines that symbolise your future life, such as a new house and what you want in it, and stick them in your notebook. Or you could create a vision board and encourage your children to make one, too. The idea is that, when you surround yourself with images of who you want to become, what you want to have, where you want to live, or even where you want to go on holiday, your life evolves to match those images and desires.

Next, make a list of your needs – both practical and emotional – and, against each one, note who can help you with it. The person you'd go to for a hug might not be the one you'd call if your car breaks down (but it's fine if it is!). That way, when you need help, you'll know exactly who to turn to.

Finally, make a list in your notebook of 10 things you can do to help pick yourself up when you have a bad day, such as having a candlelit bath, going for a run, losing yourself in a good book or film, going for a walk in nature or having a cup of tea with a friend. Then, when you feel low, open your book and pick an activity.

By thinking about all of this first and having a plan in place, it's not so much of a crisis when things go wrong. I'm afraid you're likely to have a few bad days before your divorce is finished. Preparing for the tougher days in advance means you'll be able to cope that much better.

Busting common divorce myths

Over the years, I've heard many myths about divorce, from the plausible to the downright ludicrous. Throughout this book, I'll explore some of the most common myths that I've been told, and set the record straight.

'I can't get a divorce because my spouse won't agree to one'

You can't divorce on the basis of two years' separation because that does need your spouse's consent, but a divorce based on the unreasonable behaviour of the other party is an option for everyone. We're all unreasonable at times!

'I'll wait two years to get a cheaper "quickie" divorce'

The court fee for a divorce is the same no matter what the basis of the divorce, and solicitors' fees will also be the same (unless they've gone up in the two years!).

The time it takes for a divorce to go through the court is also the same whether it's on the basis of unreasonable behaviour, adultery, or two years' separation. Therefore, I'm not sure how waiting two years can ever be considered quicker!

I believe the 'quickie' divorces we read about in the press refer to the process in court; when decree nisis are made, the judge reads out a list of names in open court. Normally, the only people to attend such court sessions are journalists (and only when a celebrity is on the list). This process of reading out the names does only take a couple of minutes, so it is indeed quick, but it's not a 'divorce'. You are only divorced when the decree absolute is granted, which only happens at least six weeks after the decree nisi.

'We need a legal separation before we can get divorced'

There's no such thing as a legal separation in England and Wales. There is no mechanism for registering your separation on any legal or formal basis. When you come to divorce, you just have to give the actual date you separated.

There is a remedy called 'judicial separation' available from the family court, which works very much like divorce, although the parties remain married at the end. This is usually used by people opposed to divorce for religious reasons.

It's possible to make a separation agreement, or deed of separation, with a solicitor prior to divorce, if you wish to formalise your arrangements. But you'd need to have a good reason for doing this. When you come to finally divorce, the separation agreement only remains valid if nothing has changed in the meantime. It's therefore usually best to go straight for financial certainty by agreeing a final financial settlement and getting the divorce process underway.

CHAPTER 2
DEALING WITH DIVORCE LAWYERS

Information really is power in divorce, but exactly what information do you need, and when? And which information applies to everyone (so can be found online or in books) and which is specific to you and your individual circumstances? Being clear about this before you rush to a solicitor can save you a lot of money.

How much money can you afford to spend on legal advice? If you have limited funds, you need to budget so that you don't run out of money towards the end of the process, which is when most people need legal advice and drafting of legal documents. This means not paying a solicitor to do things you don't actually need or can do yourself.

For instance, there's no need to pay a solicitor to complete and file your divorce petition for you. As you'll see in Chapter 7, it's easy enough to do yourself. However, there are certain circumstances where urgent legal advice is an absolute must.

When you need urgent legal advice

Don't delay in seeking legal advice if you're worried about actions your spouse might take. If in doubt, seek advice before you take any action.

For example, it will be too late to ask:

- What to do about the joint account when s/he's already emptied and spent it.

- How to get him/her out of the house and/or get it sold as soon as possible when you've already moved out.
- About the children's passports when s/he's already taken them, and possibly even taken the children abroad.
- Which jurisdiction (country) is the best one for you when your spouse has already issued a divorce petition in the best one for them.

What's more, if you want to use collaborative law, you both need to instruct a collaborative solicitor from the outset. It will usually be too late if your spouse has instructed someone else, as they're unlikely to be willing to change.

Understanding how solicitors charge

Solicitors charge an hourly rate plus VAT. Hourly rates can vary between about £150 and £950, depending on where in the country they are and how senior the solicitor dealing with your matter is. In the South East, where I'm based, you would normally expect to pay somewhere between £200 and £400 per hour. The hour is divided into six units of 10 minutes each and you'll never be charged less than one unit. So, if you were to make a two-minute phone call to a solicitor charging £250 per hour, they'll charge you for 10 minutes (around £50). The time spent on every letter or email they write to or for you will also be charged.

If your resources are limited, being aware of the costs should help to ensure you don't fall into the trap of believing that your solicitor is your friend to whom you can relay every detail of your ongoing crisis and turn to for a shoulder to cry on. A counsellor will charge you about £50 for a whole hour, rather than just 10 minutes, and they're professionally trained to deal with your grief and anger, whereas most solicitors are not. Even if you can afford to cry on your solicitor's shoulder at £200+ per hour, they need to retain their objectivity and not get too involved in your emotional issues if they're going to be able to give you the best legal advice throughout your case.

Making the most of your solicitor's time

It's important that you're crystal clear as to what you want to get from any dealing with a solicitor. The best way to do this is to write it down; it's easy to think we know exactly what we want, but when we have to write it down, it soon becomes obvious that maybe we weren't so clear after all! Take your list to your meeting with your solicitor, and make sure you write down the answers to your questions, and that you fully understand the answers at the time (so you don't have to call back for clarification).

Make sure your questions really are legal questions that can only be answered by a solicitor. If they're procedural questions, i.e. relating to form-filling, you can probably find the answer online. If your question is financial, would an accountant be a better (and cheaper) person to ask? Who else could answer your questions?

The better you can prepare for your meeting, the more value for money you'll get from it. The first thing to do is to make a note of all your basic personal details on one sheet of paper to give to your solicitor, as this will save a lot of time during your appointment. Include:

- Your full name and date of birth
- The full names and dates of birth of your spouse and children
- Your address, email and phone numbers
- Your spouse's address (if different to yours)
- The occupations of both you and your spouse
- The date of your marriage, and, if you've already split up, the date of your separation

To save further time, you can take with you two completed copies (one by you and one by your spouse) of Form E, which covers your financial situations (see also Chapter 6).

If you go to a solicitor without a copy of your spouse's Form E, your solicitor will write to your spouse, or his/her solicitor, asking for the form. It may take up to three months (sometimes more) for your spouse to complete the form, as it's so long and detailed. In the meantime, many chasing letters might be written at a cost of £50 per letter. How many letters can you afford?

Plus, you won't get much advice from your solicitor – who has an expensive insurance policy to worry about and can't afford to give you wrong advice – until they've seen a Form E from both parties.

Therefore, if you're going to a solicitor, do your Form E (and have your spouse do their Form E) first. It will save you a huge amount of time and money to have this sorted out before your first appointment. Please see Chapter 6 for more information on this important document.

If you're not comfortable completing Form E before seeing a solicitor, simply make a list of the following and take it with you to your first meeting:

- All joint assets (value of your house, car, etc.)
- All joint liabilities (outstanding mortgage, loans, etc.)
- All the assets and debts in each of your individual names
- Both of your incomes from all sources

Before your meeting with your solicitor, think carefully about how much you need to tell them. Instead of recounting a long story about your spouse's behaviour, which will have no effect at all on the financial outcome of your divorce, spend some time reducing your account to one sentence or two at the most; remember, it's advice, not sympathy, you're going for. Focus on the events leading up to the breakdown of your relationship that are most relevant to the legal questions you need answers to.

Dress for your meeting as though you're going to meet your bank manager to ask for a large loan, i.e. suited and booted. This will help create a 'business meeting' mindset, rather than a 'visit to a counsellor' mindset.

If you can, take a friend or family member with you, as two heads are usually better than one (but three or more's a crowd). Ask them to make as many notes as they can of what your solicitor tells you, as it'll be a lot to take in and you won't remember it all afterwards. They can also prompt you if they know you've forgotten to ask one of your questions. And they may be quicker to spot another question that arises from the information you're given.

Finally, remember that any decision you make in haste or in a fragile emotional state can cost you a lot of money in legal fees. Therefore, before you agree to the solicitor taking any action on your behalf, ask for time to carefully consider everything you've been told.

How to choose a solicitor

Personal recommendation is always the best way. And that means a recommendation of an individual solicitor, not a firm. Just because your parents had a great solicitor who wrote their wills doesn't mean that firm's family solicitors will be equally good.

If you're going to be using a solicitor for anything more than advising on your financial agreement and drafting it into a court document, it's really important to choose the right person.

You can change solicitor if you're not happy, but you'll incur extra costs and, the more work that's been done, the harder it'll be for a new solicitor to take over. Also, it's not uncommon for solicitors to move firms, which means you'll face the difficulty of another solicitor taking over your file (although at least you won't incur the extra cost). Sometimes solicitors have to leave without telling their clients, because the firm doesn't want them to take all their clients with them. If you liked your original solicitor and would prefer to stick with them, it's worth doing a Google search to find out which firm they've gone to, and then contacting them to see if you can move with them to their new firm.

The law is complicated and you really need a solicitor who specialises exclusively in family law. And many solicitors specialise further within family law, so you may be better off choosing a solicitor who specialises in your main problem, whether that's children law, the financial settlement (some solicitors further specialise in 'big money' cases), domestic abuse, international law, etc.

Unless you want a long and expensive fight with your ex, make sure your solicitor is a member of Resolution (www.resolution.org.uk), as they subscribe to a code of practice promoting a conciliatory approach to separation and divorce. Unfortunately, some solicitors join Resolution just so they can get more client referrals, so membership is not an absolute guarantee, but the majority of Resolution members strongly believe in the conciliatory approach. Membership of a Resolution and/or Law Society Family Panel is the sign of a more dedicated solicitor.

Some of the best solicitors are collaborative lawyers, as they've done extra training (see Chapter 1). If you're going to court for a dispute over your children, you may be better off with a solicitor who is children law accredited. If you can't agree anything with your ex, there's nothing to stop you having one solicitor for your children proceedings and one for your financial case, as they are separate proceedings at different times.

Before making your choice, you could ring a few solicitors and ask them questions such as:

- Do you specialise in family law?
- What is your main area of expertise within family law?
- What is your hourly rate?
- Who else will be working on my case, and do they have a different hourly rate?
- What will you do to try and settle my case?
- How long will my divorce take and will you be around until the end?
- Can I speak to any of your recent clients?

What will my solicitor do (and what can I do myself)?

Many people think that a solicitor has to handle the whole divorce process and all negotiations for them. But, as we see in this section, that's not the case.

What to expect of a solicitor

As we saw in Chapter 1, when clients come to me, I suggest they start by sorting out the other issues first, i.e. their parenting plan and financial settlement, before thinking about a divorce petition.

Typically, though, when you go to a solicitor, one of the first things they'll do for you is issue a divorce petition. That means filling in a form you could easily do yourself. Obviously, though, if you prefer not to do it yourself, a solicitor will do it for you at a cost of between £200 and £2,000. Many solicitors will charge a fixed fee for the divorce itself as it's a simple, procedural job and they know exactly what they're getting into.

When it comes to your financial settlement, you should tell your solicitor what you would like to achieve in your divorce (e.g. being able to stay in the house) and ask their advice as to whether this is possible and what your options are.

Once you have that advice, you can start on your chosen process (see Chapter 1) to negotiate your financial agreement. You'll be in a position of power because you have a good idea as to what you're entitled to and what options you have.

Many people choose not to take legal advice at this early stage and much will depend on your own particular circumstances. For many, it's enough to go to a solicitor with all the facts and figures on a piece of paper for a one-off session for some general advice and to be pointed in the right direction. You can get further advice from your solicitor at any time during your negotiations. Alternatively, you may be able to get free advice from a Citizens Advice Bureau (CAB) or law centre.

When you've reached agreement with your spouse on all your financial and property matters, one of you needs to ask your solicitor to draw up a consent order, which puts your agreement into legal terms. This is the time in your divorce when you absolutely do need a solicitor. Drafting this court order correctly is a complex legal task – unlike much of the work involved in the divorce itself, which is straightforward form-filling.

Please make sure you budget enough money for this vital order. It's likely to cost you at least £250 plus VAT (for a fixed-fee service), and could be up to £2,000 plus VAT depending on the complexity of your financial circumstances, and how much preparatory work you can do yourself.

If you really can't afford this fee, you can try writing your own agreement and sending it in to the court, together with your Statement of Information (Form D81). Then cross all your fingers and toes and pray that it will be picked up by a kind and helpful judge who will list it for a hearing you can attend, when they will draft it for you. Not all judges will do this, but the court does have a duty to help litigants in person, and you will have paid some hefty court fees, so it's worth a try.

Solicitors train for years to be able to draft court orders, as there are many things which have to be considered and correctly worded to produce the intended effect. If you needed brain surgery, you (hopefully) wouldn't accept if your dentist offered to do it, even if it cost you a lot less and you didn't have to wait as long. Your consent order is similarly another skilled job where you really do need the right professional to do it. As well as being trained and experienced, your solicitor will be well insured. This is important because, if they were to get something wrong, the error could cost you a lot of money and you'd want to be able to sue them.

I've had too many clients come to me when they've sacked their solicitor having spent £5,000 or £6,000 and got nowhere; maybe a divorce petition's been issued, a lot of letters have been written and a Form E might have been started or even finished.

The worst thing is, such clients are only just reaching the point where they actually need legal advice. It upsets me when this happens because I could have got them to that point for a fraction of the cost, and they would still have had money left to pay for a solicitor to give advice and draft the consent order at the end.

One solicitor is essential for drafting the consent order, though it's best if you each have a solicitor to advise you on whether the order is right for each of you. Beware, though, some solicitors will want to pull your carefully reached agreement to pieces so they can make more money. Others will have your best interests at heart when making alternative suggestions.

When a solicitor makes suggestions on your financial arrangement, make sure you understand what's being said to you so you can make your own decision. Your solicitor will know the law better than you do, but not your family, your circumstances, or your feelings. Listen carefully to their advice, but don't make any hasty decisions. If it doesn't feel right to you, don't just go along with it. Make sure you're clear as to why they made those recommendations, and what other options you may have. Don't be hurried or bullied into making a decision; talk it over with a trusted friend, family member or maybe your accountant, as you will have to live with this agreement for the rest of your life. If necessary, ask another solicitor for a second opinion.

You may find that your solicitor insists you should fight for what they believe you're entitled to, when you would be happy to settle for less money in exchange for a faster end to the divorce proceedings (or a better ongoing relationship with your ex, less trauma for your children, less to pay in legal fees, or greater peace of mind, etc.). Always remember that you're the client and you don't have to accept all the advice you're given.

However, sometimes people choose not to fight for the wrong reasons, whether through fear or guilt or something similar. Be clear and honest with yourself as to why you're not pursuing a recommended course of action. And make sure you listen regularly to that small voice within.

The 'unbundling' option

Many solicitors have caught on to the fact that you have a choice of services, as well as lots of free information on the internet, and are now offering 'pay as you go' type services that are rather unglamorously called 'unbundling'. This means that you can get legal services from the solicitor just as and when you need them, rather than having them do everything for you. You may just want some advice, or you may want help with drafting some of the court documents, but not others.

If you don't want full representation by a solicitor, you need to make sure they don't put themselves on the court record. For example, if they send a document, such as a divorce petition, to the court on your behalf, they will then be recorded by the court as acting for you and all future correspondence from the court will be sent to them, rather than to you. You then have to pay them for a postbox service where they receive documents from the court and forward them on to you.

The other thing a solicitor will do as part of full representation is to reply to the correspondence from your spouse's solicitor. This may not all be necessary; a lot of the matters dealt with in correspondence are common sense or practical issues rather than legal matters. With an unbundling service, you can reply to these letters yourself, just taking advice from your solicitor for anything you don't understand or aren't sure about.

Not all solicitors offer unbundling and even some that say they do don't really, so make sure you check out carefully with them exactly what they will and won't do, how they'll do it, and how they'll charge you. Agree this is in writing between you and the solicitor, so you're both clear as to what's included and what isn't. For example, if you're asking them to draft a financial agreement you've reached in mediation in a form acceptable to the court, are you expecting them to advise you on your agreement, or just do the drafting?

If necessary, you may need to find another solicitor who does offer exactly what you want.

Understanding litigants in person and McKenzie Friends

Legal fees have risen out of all proportion to most people's ability to be able to afford them. I've heard more than one solicitor say they wouldn't be able to afford their own fees if they got divorced! So, when it comes to court hearings, there are now more and more people who are 'litigants in person', also referred to as 'self-representing', whereas 20 years ago, they were a rare phenomenon. Solicitors, barristers and judges have all had to get better at dealing with litigants in person, but they'd really rather not, so you need to be prepared for varying receptions if you do decide to go it alone in court.

Unfortunately, some of the professionals can be horribly rude and aggressive, and solicitors will rarely speak to an unrepresented spouse on the phone, which can make it hard to get things done prior to a hearing, or when there are no court proceedings. But if you are a litigant in person, you shouldn't refuse to speak to the other party's lawyer prior to a hearing (unless they are truly objectionable). It's natural to be distrustful of them, but the judge will want to see some dialogue, at least to identify the areas of agreement and disagreement between you. But don't be bullied, and remember that having someone with you is always a good idea.

If you do need to attend a court hearing, say for a financial or children order, the first hearing will usually be a directions hearing so, if you read up about these and know what to expect, you won't find it too difficult to go by yourself. Or you could take a McKenzie Friend with you. This is someone who goes into court with you to help you present your own case. They're not usually allowed to speak for you but they can help with your paperwork and prompt you quietly with things to say. They can be a friend or relative (but never one of your children, however old they are), and should normally be allowed into court with you. However, the other party can object and the judge may refuse to let your McKenzie Friend in, for instance, if they're a potential witness, or if they're known to be partisan. If possible, notify the other party in advance, in writing (take a copy to court with you), of who will be accompanying you and that they'll be going into court with you. The judge will usually be sympathetic, if there's been no objection ahead of the hearing, but turning up without notice with a relative who your spouse dislikes intensely is not the best idea!

You also have the option of a professional McKenzie Friend, who will obviously be able to give you more help and guidance, though, of course, you'll have to pay them. So far, professional McKenzie Friends remain unregulated, but The Society of Professional McKenzie Friends Ltd has been set up to provide some self-regulation. They have a list of members, plus their hourly rates, on their website (www. mckenziefriends.directory) if you'd like to find a professional McKenzie Friend for a court hearing.

Direct access barristers

When it comes to a difficult or final hearing, you may well want to be represented in court. A barrister charges a fixed fee for a court hearing, whereas a solicitor will charge their hourly rate, so will usually be more expensive. Barristers spend most of their time in court so are typically the more experienced advocates, whereas solicitors do most of the paperwork. Solicitors will often represent clients for the earlier directions hearings (which are more straightforward) and then instruct a barrister for the more complex final hearing(s). Solicitors always used to attend court with the barrister but the cost has now become so prohibitive that they usually don't. If money is an issue for you, do check that your solicitor is not intending to go too.

Previously, barristers could only be instructed by solicitors, just as you can only go to a consultant at the hospital when your GP refers you. But now, you're allowed to go directly to some barristers, and this process is called 'direct access' or sometimes 'public access'. This is an excellent, cost-effective option for many people whose cases are relatively straightforward or if you only require representation for part of the process.

You'll need to pick your barrister carefully. Find one who specialises in family law and, if your case is at all complex, one who specialises in the area of your dispute: usually children or finances. If you have a dispute in both of these areas, these will be separate proceedings, and you may wish to have a different barrister for each. Their profiles will be on the website of their chambers (a barrister's office), making it easier to find one that's right for you. All barristers have a clerk who you will have to deal with first, and negotiate a fee with.

Some direct access barristers will help you with some of the paperwork for your court hearing, while others will expect you to do it yourself if you don't have a solicitor. You should discuss with the clerk what level of support you're looking for.

Paying for legal fees: Legal aid and litigation loans

Unless you're the victim of domestic violence and meet strict criteria, there's no longer any legal aid for divorce or related matters, although, if you're on benefits or a very low income, you may be exempt from some of the court fees.

Your solicitor may accept monthly payments throughout your case, if those payments are likely to cover your total fees, but not all solicitors are willing to do this.

You may be able to get a loan from your bank, depending on your circumstances, and possibly on your solicitor's willingness to give an undertaking to the bank assuring them that the loan will be repaid at the end of the case.

Alternatively, family or friends may offer you a loan to cover your legal fees. If it really is a loan (and not a gift), which you will have to repay, make sure you have a proper loan agreement drawn up. You can either get your solicitor to do it, or find a template agreement on the internet. This not only gives clarity to your lender, as well as to you, but you can then put it on your Form E as one of your liabilities and it will be taken into account in your final settlement.

There are two companies, Novitas and Iceberg, which give loans through solicitors for family litigation where the matrimonial home or other property will be sold at the end of the proceedings, enabling the loan to be repaid then. In the meantime, both charge interest (currently at 18% pa).

If all else fails, and your spouse has money and you don't, it's been possible since April 2013 to apply to the court for a Legal Services Order. If granted, your spouse would have to make payments for your legal fees. You may or may not have to repay this money at the end of your case, depending on the outcome.

Busting common divorce myths

When it comes to working with solicitors, there's one myth repeated by many anxious spouses:

'I don't have a choice. My spouse has a solicitor and/or started court proceedings so I have to get a solicitor, too'

You do have a choice as to whether or not you instruct a solicitor. Don't be panicked into rushing off to one just because you've received a solicitor's letter or court papers. All it means is that your spouse has paid the court fee and a lot of money to their solicitor to issue the proceedings. If you can hold your nerve, and if your spouse has a good solicitor, you can leave them to do most of the work for you as well!

CHAPTER 3
DEALING WITH
THE EMOTIONAL FALLOUT

Divorce can feel like riding on a roller coaster without a safety bar, and with a pit of fire burning underneath, so staying positive is a huge challenge. But, particularly if you have children, it's a challenge you'll do your best to rise to. You're bound to have the odd meltdown, but if you can have them when the children aren't around, you'll protect them from some of your rawest emotions. Of course, it's fine for the kids to see you're sad at times, and they'll be confused if you're constantly putting a brave face on and pretending everything is great. Your children will be sad too, but they tend to show their feelings more in their behaviour than emotional outbursts. Children bounce back more quickly than adults, and they still need to have fun, even though it may be the last thing you feel like doing.

This may seem a strange question if you didn't want to separate, but what are the benefits of your separation? Try to list five benefits in your notebook, as this list will help you to stay positive on a bad day. Your list may include things like not having to cook meals at a certain time, having a whole bed to yourself, always being able to watch what you want on TV, having less shopping to do, having a quieter house, whatever works for you.

Don't create your future life while standing on your head

Divorce is an emotional, if not traumatic, process resulting in huge practical changes, many financial consequences, and a few legal consequences. For many, it's a huge shock too. This has an effect on your brain, your body and your spirit, and you're unlikely to be in any fit state to make big decisions regarding the rest of your life. So, with all this going on, it's not only strange that a solicitor is usually the first port of call, it can also be an expensive mistake.

To put it another way, if your friend's husband had just died, would you immediately start talking to her about her pension plan? Of course not. We all have a fear of endings of any kind, and divorce is said to be even worse than bereavement because, as well as losing your spouse and your dreams for the future, there are probably feelings of rejection or betrayal to deal with. So, be kind to yourself. Treat yourself the way you would the friend who just lost her husband.

I often liken it to being turned upside down and then set back on your feet again. You may look okay, but your brain's going to take longer to settle down and function normally again. It's not a time to be doing much thinking, so you need to take care of only the absolute essentials in your life while you work out which way is up.

Sara's story

Sara was angry and upset when her partner left her, and their two children, for one of her friends. She coped by 'living in the moment', so, if she felt sad, she would cry her eyes out and wallow in the feelings until they passed. She did a lot of dancing (this is a good therapy, akin to animals shaking themselves after a trauma) and swimming, which she said felt like all the hurt and anger being washed away. She recovered, and was soon looking radiant – much more quickly than others who try to avoid their emotions.

When your head feels a little more settled, you may want to consider some counselling. Relate offers counselling for couples who are separating as well as those who want to stay together. Otherwise, if you can afford it, it's a good idea to find a counsellor to support you individually through the process. What other support can you get for yourself, perhaps from friends, family or support groups? You can't have too much support at this time. Remember, you're dealing with a situation worse than a bereavement, so think about what you would expect a friend in that position to want and need.

When one spouse has been thinking about separating for a long time, but it comes as a shock to the other party, it can leave them 'playing emotional catch-up'. This is when solicitors' fees escalate; if you're not capable of making rational decisions because you're still in shock, you can end up in court before you know it – which may not be what either of you wanted. Worse still is when one spouse discovers the other is having an affair; one's in shock, the other's in love, so neither is capable of making good long-term decisions. It's best not to rush to solicitors too soon in these situations.

One difference between divorce and bereavement is that you usually have more time before any practical action is needed; you don't have to rush to arrange a funeral, and then get probate sorted out before the tax man comes knocking on your door. You may well feel overwhelmed by the number of things you need to do, but nothing happens fast in a divorce. Our legal system is creaking at the seams and grinding to a halt, so take a deep breath, then another, and do things in your own time. This doesn't mean putting things off – after all, they won't go away. It means having a plan and a list that you can work steadily through. You'll get there, taking it one gentle step at a time.

If the court has issued a timetable in children or financial proceedings, you'll have to keep to that. If you don't meet a deadline, the court may then order you to do something in a very short time indeed. If you're really struggling to comply with a deadline, ask the other party to agree to give you more time; they won't do themselves any favours if they object to reasonable requests. Also, when you're agreeing a timetable, whether with your solicitor or the other party or their lawyer, which may be at court, make sure it's a realistic one. If you're planning a holiday or know there will be particular pressure at work, factor that in rather than panic when you can't comply with the timetable. Sometimes, however, you'll just have to comply, even if that does mean making some sacrifices.

Coping with disbelief: Catch the thought

When we're facing something traumatic in life, our minds tend to go into overdrive and some of our thoughts can loop round and round. And, when you're dealing with something this difficult, you need to get everything possible working for, rather than against, you. Your thoughts are powerful. If you're able to tame them, they really can help you to feel better.

What is the thought that's going round and round in your head right now? There'll be loads of them, but usually there's a dominant one such as 'this can't be happening' or 'I don't believe it' or 'I can't cope with this'. Thoughts like this will confuse your brain, which can see that it has indeed happened and that you are coping. You need to be as clear-headed as possible during this time, as there'll be enough confusion from outside. Take time to listen to your thoughts until you manage to identify the most frequent one. Then, change it into its positive opposite, which could be something like 'it's happened and I can cope'. Find words which sit well with you, and then repeat them to yourself like a mantra hundreds of times a day. Each time you find yourself with a negative thought, repeat your mantra a few times. You may need more than one. 'This too will pass' is a soothing one for difficult times. And, for some people, 'I forgive you and I let you go' is a helpful one.

What colour is your front door? If you visualised your door and came up with an answer, you'll understand how the brain always has to answer questions, even if only to yourself. So, instead of saying to yourself 'I can't' or 'I'm scared', ask yourself something like 'how can I find the courage to…?' Your brain will search for answers for you, which is more constructive than just shutting it down. But, beware questions starting with 'why', which can be disempowering. Instead of asking 'why is this happening?' you could try 'what do I want to do now?'

Finding the help you need

This is an extremely stressful time and you're going to have some sleepless nights when the stress hormones don't stop flooding your body at bedtime. As shown before, try and catch the thought that's going round in your head and keeping you awake. Try not to fret about not sleeping. You have enough to worry about already and it's not realistic to expect to sleep well at such a difficult time. And, as you're going to have a lot of paperwork to do, maybe you can make good use of the extra time!

That said, it's really important to look after yourself properly during all this stress so that you can stay well, not only during the divorce, but afterwards too. Unfortunately, divorce does take a heavy toll on some people's health. That's why, as well as your divorce plan, I recommend that you make a 'sanity plan'.

It's sometimes hard for us to ask for the support we need, but I can guarantee that you're going to need some. Asking for appropriate help, rather than waiting until you fall apart, shows you are coping. You will have family and friends who want to support you, but won't necessarily know what you need or when, so it's much better if you can work that out for them and let them know how best they can help.

Your needs during this time may include some of the following:

- Moral support, including hugs, shoulders to cry on and people to reassure you you're doing okay and will get through this.

- A wise and objective sounding board. Someone to bounce ideas off when you're negotiating your parenting plan and financial settlement.

- Someone who's good with figures and/or understands finance, pensions, mortgages, businesses, tax, etc.

- Childcare, particularly at times when your ex would have been there, and while you attend solicitors' appointments, mediation, etc.

- A childcare emergency contact, i.e. a neighbour or someone you can call on if you're unexpectedly delayed.

- Practical help with household tasks or repairs.

- Help with transport.

Use your notebook to make a list of your needs on one side of the page, and the names of people who can help with each need on the other.

Planning ahead like this will help when (not if!) you have an emergency, or difficult situation to deal with. You're less likely to make bad decisions if you've thought things through in advance. Working out who you can lean on will also help you avoid using your child as your confidante or support, which is a very unfair burden to place on young shoulders. Children need to feel safe and know that adults are in charge, rather than feeling responsible for their parents.

Catherine's story

I grew up in South Africa and I was 12 or 13 when my parents divorced. We lived a comfortable life in a large house – in fact, I would say we were spoilt – but I used to dread Saturdays because my mother went out drinking; she didn't tolerate alcohol that well and, if she had one too many, she would become aggressive. It would upset my father, who lived on his nerves. He would worry dreadfully if she didn't return, and would start phoning hospitals to try and find her. I did a lot of pacing up and down.

Eventually, my mother moved out of the house, although she came back to see us every day. However, at the time, I was more interested in my friends, and I do remember snubbing her. I knew my father couldn't be on his own, and he married again within a year, and took on two more children. When my stepmother moved into the house, my brother and I were forced to choose who we wanted to live with. That was really hard, although we were of an age to know our own minds and be able to make that choice. The dynamics had changed with our stepmother in our mother's house; it no longer felt like ours and there were suddenly loads of rules and regulations we had to abide by. We both chose to live with our mother, despite the fact that she was living in a very much smaller house, and she too had a new partner. My stepsisters, who were gaining a beautiful big house, didn't even wait for me to move out before taking over my room and rearranging it, and I remember crying and sobbing when I saw them in it.

At the time of the divorce I felt as though the world was coming to an end. However, you do survive! The divorce was amicable but my mother confided in me a lot, which I really didn't enjoy, and our relationship was like a role reversal. I was my mother's mother, forced to grow up quickly, always looking out for her. When she went out at night to meet her partner for a drink, I was always worried about what state she'd come home in. I spent many a night dragging her out of pubs with 'bar flies' telling me that I should smile more. I didn't have anything to smile about; I was the responsible person, always on tenterhooks, hoping that things wouldn't get out of hand, and I was often embarrassed by her behaviour. She had always worked, but never paid a bill, and I took care of those too.

Protecting my mother took its toll on me. I hid it for years, but suffered with depression as a result. At 19, I asked to see a psychologist, but I still protected my mother as she was always the victim. Eventually, when it did come out, after I was married, my husband and I decided to leave South Africa and relocate to the UK. Part of the reason for moving was to get away from my mum. I no longer wanted to feel responsible for her. It was the best thing I ever did; my mum was forced to stand on her own two feet and learn to do things for herself.

I wanted my mother to be a mother that would love and nurture me. Instead, I had to be the responsible person in the relationship. I realise now, years later, that my mother was doing the best she could with the resources she had. She's always been co-dependent on others.

My brother and I had to go to our dad's every other weekend, which we didn't enjoy. We were made to feel guilty, as Dad and his wife kept telling us how they couldn't afford things with four children to pay for.

My parents would tolerate each other and weren't rude per se. My mother used to complain that 'your father doesn't pay me enough maintenance' but never said anything else bad about him. Now, she and my stepmother are really good friends, and my mother sometimes goes to stay with her and my father. I've even heard my father introduce the two of them as 'this is my wife, and this is my ex-wife'!

Looking back, things could have been better for my brother and me if my parents had thought through the consequences of their separation and realised the huge impact it would have on their children. It would also have helped if we all could have truly expressed how we were feeling, although I do realise that was never going to happen in our family!

I put on a mask, suppressed my anger and carried it around for a long time, which caused me to suffer from depression. However, with the help of a lot of personal development, I've worked through it all and have no problems now.

When your spouse says they won't move out and they won't go to a solicitor

For many, this is a worst-case scenario. I've known women (and it usually is women, in my experience) get stuck for years in a situation when their husband simply won't do anything towards a separation or divorce.

The first thing to do is to have an honest conversation with yourself about why this has happened. I've known people who've been unhappy and planning to leave for years, without actually mentioning this to their spouse. Then, when they're finally ready to make their move, they're surprised that their spouse isn't too. Such people assume their spouse must have known they were unhappy, and been equally unhappy themselves, but that's often not the case. If your spouse is in shock when you've made your announcement, this 'threat' may simply be their initial response. The best thing you can do in this situation is give your spouse a little time to catch up emotionally.

Then there are those who've 'cried wolf' too many times by making threats of divorce that they'd no intention of acting on. When they do finally mean it, their spouse doesn't take them seriously and doesn't do anything. If this is the case with you and your spouse, you may need to ask a solicitor to write them a letter to convince them you do mean business this time.

If you've made it clear over a period of time that you're unhappy (by complaining about their behaviour or drinking, for example) and your spouse still refuses to co-operate when you say you want to leave, you'll need to apply for a divorce at the beginning, rather than much later in the process, as I'd normally recommend. Download a divorce petition from the internet (or get one from your local county court), fill it in, and give your spouse a copy. Ask them if they want anything changed and, if they don't give you an answer, tell them you're sending it to the court.

Most people will respond when they receive a divorce petition from the court. If they don't, you'll have to issue an application for a financial remedy on Form A. The court will then set out a timetable for your case. It's likely your spouse will attend the court hearings because they won't want to risk the court making an order giving all of the joint assets to you.

If you're really worried that your husband may be violent if you proceed in this way, you'll need to talk to a solicitor about getting an occupation order. This means your spouse has to leave the house before you start the process.

Tackling common divorce fears

Divorce can be a challenging and scary time and there are certain fears that I hear regularly. Let's explore them in detail.

'I'm too scared to divorce'

I'm not surprised you're scared. Most people are, and it'd be unusual if you weren't. Divorce is huge and probably one of the most traumatic things you'll go through in your life. So, you need to dig deep and gather your courage. The book Feel the Fear and Do it Anyway by Susan Jeffers has some useful tips for overcoming your fears. Rest assured that you will get through this difficult time, and you'll be surprised by your own abilities to tackle new or tough things.

When you're going through a divorce, it's like being in a long tunnel: you know there's light at either end of it, but, when you're in the middle, it's a dark, scary place to be. My favourite quote from Winston Churchill sums this up perfectly: 'When you're going through hell, keep going.'

Just keep putting one foot in front of the other and, eventually, you'll be out of the tunnel and in a much happier place. The longer you put off starting, the longer it'll take to get to the other side.

'I'm scared we'll get into a fight'

Our legal system is adversarial. That means you're automatically getting straight into a fight, which is a dreadful way to deal with a family breakdown. Although some of the legalese has improved, divorce cases are still referred to as 'Smith v Smith'. And, at the end of it all, Mr and Mrs Smith are expected to go away and be good parents together. It's a big ask!

It's a challenging time. Your head's in a spin, but you think you need to urgently do something about this crisis you're in. So, you rush off to see a solicitor, and you feel reassured that your solicitor will take care of it all for you. Which they will – at a price.

And that price is twofold: the money you'll spend fighting it out in court, and, if you have kids, the price your children will pay. Unless you and your spouse both go to very good solicitors, who write very careful and friendly letters, the temperature is soon going to rise and you'll be divided into two distinct camps: Smith v Smith. This is the fault of our adversarial system. Your solicitor is going to fight for what's best for you, and your spouse's solicitor is going to fight for what's best for them. And in the middle of this fight are your children. Who's going to fight for what's best for them? The very worst thing for children is parents who fight.

So, please don't rush off and engage a solicitor. Try to reach agreements between yourselves, perhaps with the help of mediators. By all means, take some initial legal advice if that will reassure you, but don't ask the solicitor to do anything at all, or pay any up-front fees, until you're absolutely sure that it's necessary. There's more on this in Chapter 2.

Meanwhile, if you've not been separated for two years and neither of you have had an affair, you may have to issue a divorce petition based on your spouse's unreasonable behaviour. You probably don't need me to tell you that this is unlikely to go down well. So, wherever possible, try to communicate with your spouse about what you'll be putting in the divorce petition. It may help them to remember that the 'unreasonable behaviour' ground is merely a means to an end.

There are other things you can do on a more personal level to smooth the process and minimise conflict and distress. Take the moral high ground whenever you can. Pick your moment for a difficult conversation; ask your spouse when's the best time to talk so that they're prepared and not preoccupied with something else. If you need to broach something controversial and are worried about how your spouse will react, go to a café or pub or another public place where emotions are more likely to be kept in check.

In these days of instant communication, it's easy to get swept into something you didn't intend. There's no reason to respond instantly to a text or email, so make it a rule that you sleep on it. We use a lot of shorthand in these communications, which can't convey the same tone as when we speak, so make sure you do understand what the other person meant before you respond in anger and get into a fight.

If you receive an angry message, do you really need to reply? If you're clear about your goals for your divorce, you can ask yourself if replying is going to take you any nearer to one of your objectives. If you have children, one of your objectives is likely to be that you'll end up with a good co-parenting relationship with your ex. If that's the case, you can measure your replies against that aim.

It's easy to take things too personally when navigating such a difficult journey, so it's important to ask for more information before getting upset or angry. When your spouse says 'I'm not paying for your car to be repaired next week', are they saying that to hurt you, or is it that they've run out of money and don't get paid until the week after? When your spouse says 'you can't have the children next Saturday', is that an attack on you, or have the children been invited to an exciting birthday outing, and you can have them on Sunday instead?

Unless your relationship has disintegrated into all-out warfare, when all you can do is attack each other, it helps to remember that, most of the time, the other person will be thinking more about themselves than they will about you. Asking what they need to be able to agree to your request will advance your cause better than getting angry.

If you can avoid burning your bridges with your ex, it'll serve you much better in the long run. After all, being a single parent is hard. You'll need their help and support during the years to come, and you'll be glad of some much-needed time to yourself while the children are with their other parent.

'People will judge me. I'll feel like a failure'

My definition of a failed marriage is one where neither party has learned anything. And, if you have one or more children, please don't let them hear you say your marriage is a failure!

When marriage first came about, people were lucky if they lived until they were 40. Now, we potentially have time for three long marriages in a lifetime. Our intimate relationships are where we learn and grow the most in life, but sometimes one person reaches a place where they can learn no more by staying with the other, and it's time to move on. That means the relationship has concluded, not failed. It makes me sad when people rubbish all the joy and good times they had in their relationship because it's ended now. The problem, of course, is in the marriage vows, which we make with no idea of what the future holds for us.

Rather than dwelling on your 'failed marriage', focus positively on having a successful divorce. Writing a letter to your partner may help to complete your marriage, heal any wounds, and set a good course for your future as co-parents. Here's a suggested template that you can amend to suit your circumstances:

Dear ......

Thank you for ...

and for ...

and for ...

One of my most treasured memories of our time together is ...

What I like best about you is ...

I admire you for ...

I respect you for ...

I want ...

I'm sorry that ...

I'm afraid that ...

I hope that ...

My hope for the future is that you will ...

CHAPTER 4
DEALING WITH THE CHILDREN

There are 350,000 children involved in divorce each year, and it can be as traumatising and life-changing for them as it is for their parents.

Limiting the damage to your children

They will certainly be upset for a while, but that's not a reason not to separate if there's really no saving your marriage. In fact, some children are relieved by the separation, although they may well be upset later by all the changes and by any arguments between their parents. Conflict between parents is usually more damaging to children than the separation itself, so they may be harmed more by parents who are not on good terms but stay together. When you consider the fact that you're a role model for your children, ask yourself this: are you happy with the life and relationship you're showing them?

When you're separating, your job is to keep talking to your children, reassuring them and doing all you can to limit the damage. There's no doubt that children are damaged to some degree by divorce, but they're also damaged by all sorts of other things that happen at home, at school and in the wider world.

Children can feel terribly alone when their parents separate. So far as they're concerned, the divorce is all about them: their universe has imploded. But, for their parents, it's adult business which has nothing to do with their children. This can leave the children feeling very shut out.

Children may show by their behaviour, such as bullying, self-harming or refusing to

go to school, that they're not coping with some aspect of the divorce. If you make notes on one page of your notebook, with dates, of any difficult behaviour or symptoms your child exhibits, then you can see if there's any pattern. For example, does Billy always get a tummy ache on Sunday night?

If a child is behaving really badly, it's imperative that both parents work together, maybe with a therapist, to find out what's wrong and put it right before those difficult behaviours become embedded and challenging for both parent and child to deal with. Obviously, if the parents are at loggerheads with each other this is easier said than done, but, somehow, they need to contain their battle elsewhere and come together for their child.

On the other hand, some children behave impeccably and the emotional problems they're covering up won't surface until adolescence or adulthood. Others will have physical symptoms such as pains, rashes, bedwetting or disturbed sleep. And some, even young children, may suffer from depression, which may show up in physical symptoms, or in them appearing sad or listless.

Give your children the attention they need

One of the problems with divorce is that it's all-consuming, particularly if you have property and financial arrangements to settle, as well as coping with the emotional trauma. You're suddenly a single parent and your children may be as shocked and traumatised as you are, but you've less time than ever to give to them.

Chris's story
I was 16 when the divorce started (I'm 18 now and it still hasn't been finalised). I was aware years before that there were problems. They were sleeping in separate rooms, so I knew something was up, but wasn't quite old enough to fully understand why they did that.

Rather than being upset, awfully, I felt a huge sense of relief that they were finally separating. Things hadn't been good for a long time and I knew that neither of them were happy in their marriage. I knew my dad hadn't treated my mum particularly well in the last years of their marriage, so it was good to know that she could finally be happy in the long run, even if, in the short term, it was very upsetting for her. The thing that worried me the most at that time was moving house, as I'd been living in my previous house all my life and I didn't know anything else.

I was due to change school for sixth form anyway because I'd hated my secondary school. I fitted in well at my sixth form, which was good, and made a secure circle of friends who helped me a lot through various hard times. I don't really think the divorce affected my A Levels that much, as schoolwork was an outlet to forget about what was happening at home, and so I threw myself into revising and working. My exam results were good, all things considered, and I know that I've done the best that I can. I'm off to university in September.

The divorce left me with eating issues – not a full-blown eating disorder, but I definitely have had issues over the past two years about whether my thighs are far enough apart, and becoming fixated on pictures of abnormally skinny girls with sticking out bones (that's the dark side of Tumblr for you...). I have the opposite of comfort eating – whenever I'm stressed or angry, I stop eating. I think these eating issues developed because it was a cry for attention, as my mum had been so preoccupied with the divorce, but also as a coping mechanism – whenever I felt angry, I wouldn't eat to punish myself and those around me, but also to make people look at me and give me attention. Today, I have much better coping mechanisms, like running, and immersing myself in my art. My eating issues are basically fine now, but I have had to learn not to take out my emotions on my body.

It's also made me more cynical about love and marriage, and whether marriage is really worth it, as it's so much easier to get married than to get divorced. However, I'm now in a long-term relationship, and can definitely see why marriage is so attractive, as it's a sacred bond between two people who want to make their love concrete.

The positive consequences of the divorce for me are that we've now got two beautiful brother and sister rescue cats (my dad doesn't like cats), and I've become really close with my mum and siblings, which is lovely.

Younger children can be so frightened that, as one parent has abandoned them, the other could leave too. They can drive a parent to distraction by following their every move, too scared to let them out of their sight. If constant reassurance that you love them and want nothing more than to stay with them doesn't work, you may want to consider play therapy, if your child is old enough.

Depression is a natural adult reaction to the misery of separation and divorce but it can mean that a parent is just as absent from their children's lives as they are when they're too busy fighting their ex. If you're seriously depressed, it's not possible to be an adequate single parent to your children and you must get some outside help and support.

Don't shut out grandparents and wider family

Grandparents can offer a more stable influence at this turbulent time, provided they can remain neutral and not take one of the parents' sides. Godparents, aunts and uncles, and family friends can also help the children by listening to their worries and fears, offering advice where needed, and ensuring that they have some fun.

You may not have been a big fan of your in-laws before the divorce but, if your children were fond of them, it's especially important now to maintain that bond. Grandparents form part of a child's identity and, if for any reason a child is not seeing much of one of their parents, it's even more important for them to know the parent's parents.

Don't fight in front of the kids

The most damaging thing for a child is conflict between their parents. Your child loves both of you. And, when you stop loving each other, this creates a difficult situation that you each need to manage to the very best of your ability.

Look at it from your child's point of view; up until now they've looked at the two of you together, as one unit:

And now, they find themselves in the middle of the two of you:

This is an enormous change in their life; now, when they turn to see one of you, they can't see the other, and they feel confused and frightened. Your job is to do all you can to reassure them that you both still love them just as before, and that you both always will, even though lots of things are changing. If you're fighting your ex, your child is in the middle of your fight, feeling frightened and not knowing which way to turn.

Dibley's story

I was three years old when my parents separated and I remember standing between them shouting 'stop screaming at each other'.

They blamed each other for affecting their son, both during and after their rows. The conflict between them made me feel insecure – whatever it was wasn't necessary. It was disturbing, especially when my mother started crying. She gave as good as she got, but the constant blaming bothered me.

It was clear that I would live with my mother, but I saw my father a few times a week. He usually came to our house but I sometimes went to his place. The arrangement was better for me in that the fighting reduced dramatically, although there were always points of contention. But it was not better in that I missed Dad, and he became the good guy.

At the time, you don't appreciate the person who's actually taking care of you, just the other one who is the good guy, who you can't afford to upset. So, in that respect, the divorce worked out well for him.

When a united front is not presented, a child is confused. This resulted in me thinking more for myself at an early age. My mother would say one thing, and my father the opposite. So, I would do neither, in order that they didn't think I preferred the other one. If they agreed with each other, I'd still disagree sometimes because I'd given myself permission not to agree with them. As a result, I made lots of mistakes that could have been avoided if I'd been more open to parental guidance.

It was their divorce that formed me, and not necessarily for the better. I became a rebel flying the flag, a free-thinking individual. I became somewhat isolated as I didn't think that my peers would listen to me (just as I didn't listen to my parents), and I bullied other children at primary school. I was not a happy child and got into fights at school.

The divorce has had an adverse effect on my relationships as an adult. I lack belief in the dynamic and, as soon as things start to go wrong, I'm out. I'm on a short fuse and I have no tolerance or patience for bickering, blaming, or judgement. Had my parents not divorced, my relationship in my 20s may have worked because my attitude would have been different. She was the love of my life. I still love her, although she is married to someone else and I have no contact with her.

I have a fear of abandonment, which makes me abandon women quickly so they can get over it easily – but if I wait six years and then they were to abandon me, I may never get over it. Sometimes my fear makes me hold tight to people and sometimes it makes me push them away.

From the age of 10, my father was not there. Then he showed up thinking he could make up for lost time; but no, that ship had sailed. My mother was the source of constant help, always there. My father is my father by name, by title, nothing more.

My mother bad-mouthed my father a lot, but my father never spoke badly of her. I used to disagree with her as a child, which only made her do it more. When I stopped disagreeing, she stopped the bad-mouthing and then went to the other extreme, telling me I should see him because he's still my father. And it was she who organised for us to meet again after I had not wanted to see him for many years.

Do all you can to keep your anger and distress out of your conversations with your children; they won't ask questions or tell you what's worrying them if they think it'll upset or anger you. But, you're human, and probably upset and frightened yourself, so you're going to get it wrong sometimes. When that happens, just apologise to your child as soon as you can, explain that you're upset or angry, and that sometimes we say things we don't mean in the heat of the moment. Reassure them that it's not their fault and that you shouldn't have said or done what you did. You're a role model for your child, so see it as an opportunity to model the behaviour you'd like to see in them when they make a mistake.

Children often want their parents to get back together again. They may need to hear the message, very gently, from each of you that that's not going to happen, to enable them to move on from their fantasy and deal with the reality of their situation.

One of the worst things you can do to your child is to bad-mouth their other parent; putting down the other parent will never enhance you but it may damage your relationship with your child. You may have fallen out of love with your ex, but your children haven't. They still love, want and need both of their parents just as much as before and it's cruel to try to change that.

Jo's story

I was eight years old when my parents divorced. The night my mum told my dad that she didn't want to be with him, I remember being woken by shouting and screaming. My mum went downstairs and my dad followed. It was very emotional and I remember crying in my bed; my mum came and got in with me.

After that, I remember a series of arguments and blame. There were particular arguments where my dad was violent and I witnessed him throwing my mum across the room one evening. He came in the house wanting something from Mum's handbag. I just remember holding the bag and hiding under the table. He would let himself into the house, drunk and angry. It was scary as he didn't seem to care what we saw or heard as children.

Another night, my mum received a warning call from a friend and we were packed into the car and taken to my aunt's for the night. But, as we were driving off, my dad came back and kicked the car and dented the door. I just remember it being scary and I had to protect my mum.

After we moved to a new house with Mum, Dad bribed us. He said, if we went and lived with him, we could have the lifestyle

Mum couldn't afford for us. I regretted my decision as soon as I said goodbye to Mum and remember crying on the bed. Dad was still very angry and would make obnoxious comments about Mum; he said that she didn't care about us, she had a new life without us now and didn't care about seeing us. I would defend Mum and this would just make him angry. He would threaten to take my horse away and stop me from going to see him. If Mum came to collect us from the house, Dad would go outside and start an argument with her; Mum had to get a restraining order and we would have to walk to the bottom of the road to be picked up and dropped off, which was a relief as it avoided the confrontation.

Although I did get on better with Dad as I got older, I stopped communicating with him when I was in my 20s as I realised that he wasn't a dad. He didn't behave like a dad or what I thought a dad should be. I still feel now that I made the right decision, although I would not rule out ever speaking with him, but I wouldn't welcome him back as my dad. When I got married, he didn't give me away and wasn't invited to the wedding. I don't have much communication with Dad's side of my family because I chose not to speak to my dad, so they were not invited either. This saddens me, but I am privileged to have an amazing circle of friends; people say you can't choose your family but I believe you can.

You may have all sorts of uncharitable feelings about your child's other parent, but this is adult business. I know it's tempting to try and get your child 'on your side', but the reality is that your child, more than ever before, needs to know that both their parents are on their side. The question to ask yourself is this: whose needs are more important, mine or my child's?

You'll have all sorts of emotions hurtling around inside you, sometimes all at the same time. You'll feel angry with your ex and want to get back at them – or grief-stricken that they've gone, and want to get them back. You'll feel scared about your future and need reassurance yourself. You'll be sad about the end of your relationship, and need a shoulder to cry on. Don't be tempted to use your children for any of these purposes. Being a parent is always a tough job, but, right now, it's harder than ever. What's being asked of you at this difficult time is to step up and be a better parent than ever.

However, although you may think now that you'll feel anger towards your ex forever, you can work through your feelings and come to a place of peace with it all. And when you reach that point, you don't want to have regrets about how you treated your child at this time. You'll be much better able to do the right thing for your child if you get help for yourself to process your feelings.

Take it slow with new partners

People often want to introduce their children to their new partner far too soon. This needs to be done at the child's pace, rather than their parent's. The Centre for Separated Families recommends waiting two years before introducing new partners. Children need this time to process the separation and divorce, and it also gives the new partner the best chance of being accepted by the children and having a good relationship with them.

When it's your ex who has a new partner, it's always likely to be too soon for you; you may not ever be happy (unless maybe your ex's parenting skills are somewhat lacking, in which case, you may feel relieved there's someone else around). Your children won't share your uncharitable view of your ex, however. Seeing their parent with a new partner may be tough for them to deal with, and they'll need all the help you can give them to cope.

It certainly doesn't help them if you tell them how dreadful your ex's new partner is, and then send them off to visit or live with them. If you find it too difficult to talk and listen to your children about this, you could consider counselling or play/art therapy for them, and support or therapy for yourself.

If it's you who has a new partner, you're likely to be in love and happy, but your children may still be reeling from the shock of their family splitting apart, and certainly not ready to see one of their parents canoodling with a stranger or to witness your joy with the stranger who's replaced a beloved parent. Enjoy your new-found happiness, but give your children the time to adjust slowly to any new relationship.

Jules's story

My parents separated when I was 17 (during my AS levels). Their relationship hadn't been great for two or three years; communication had broken down and I recognise now that that my mother's dependence on my father caused resentment. Prior to their separation, I would pick up on the fact that they would not show any signs of affection towards one another, they would often ignore each other and there would be exchanges of unpleasantness. The animosity in the house was extremely distressing and hard to cope with. Witnessing sadness and bad feeling still makes me tearful now.

I was distraught and upset by the unpleasant exchanges between my parents. Knowing that my parents had spoken to each other in such a way to harm each other's feelings was extremely upsetting, especially when I had strong feelings for each of them. This still affects me now in that, both in previous relationships and with my current partner, I tend not to like swearing, or raised voices.

Arguments would often ensue from the 'state of the house', with my mother being accused of being lazy. To make matters easier for both of them, I'd often compulsively clean the house (which is something I do now in my own flat if I am feeling low and want to make myself feel better).

In the months leading to the separation, my father was progressively absent. I understood he would stay at work and, each time he did come home, he would remove something to take with him. Eventually, on her birthday, my mother told me they were separating. She was very apologetic, yet composed, but I was distraught and felt as though my life had split in two.

I was deeply concerned about my mother's financial position and my dad's financial and mental wellbeing. My father had previously had a bad time at work, had had depression and had subsequently been drinking a lot. I did feel sorry for my father and recall crying about it quite a lot. Luckily, I was able to talk to my friends and other close family members around me at the time, such as my mother's mum and her sisters. We had a family dog and he was a big comfort. My AS levels were not great. However, I managed to undertake re-sits the following year to achieve As. It may be likely the divorce played a hand in this, but other factors could have contributed.

My brother, sister and I stayed with my mother. We would have to make the arrangements to see my father, as he never really was that forthcoming. I don't believe my brother (who fell out with my father) or my sister (due to her age) stayed in contact with him at that point, so I felt alone in that respect. I think sometimes I felt disconnected from my father, given his prolonged absence in the run up to the separation. He was with another woman fairly swiftly after my mother had informed me of the breakup, which was a shock. It didn't affect my relationship with my father, as I knew he was happier and he was entitled to that. I understood that his relationship with my mother was not good and it would have been selfish for me to want them to remain together.

Prior to my studies, I had to move in with my father and his partner and, during this period, she fell pregnant. Being informed of this was extremely hard. It felt as though it was another nail in the coffin of the breakup of the family unit. Although I was made to feel included, he had a new family. I also recall being asked by his partner when I was moving out. Although I had made plans to do so, I did feel hurt.

Unfortunately, my mother has not found a long-term partner, but she has met several guys over the last few years. She would often drop us to go on dates or disappear without mention, which left me feeling extremely worried and concerned.

As a result of the divorce, I am perhaps more independent than I would otherwise have been. I am reluctant to rely on a man emotionally and financially, and am driven to support myself, hence the reason why I have pursued a career in law (not, of course, being the only reason).

I have a good relationship with my parents now, although they still tend to make snipey comments about one another, which I don't entertain. I wouldn't hold it against my father for leaving as they were both unhappy – at least he did something to change the situation. My stepmother is lovely and very accommodating. I acknowledge that the relationship is something that I shouldn't stick my nose into or perhaps voice an opinion about. I'm pleased I've been able to take a step back and remain impartial. Unfortunately, my older brother hasn't done the same, which has meant he has jeopardised his relationship with his father. They haven't spoken now for several years and my brother has never met his three-year-old stepbrother, who is a real sweetheart.

Maintain boundaries

Boundary setting can be a challenge; when you're new to single parenthood, exhausted, under the weather or preoccupied, it's easier just to let a child continue to sit quietly in front of the TV rather than embark on a battle to enforce bedtime. And, after all, the worst that's likely to result from going to bed a little later one day is a grumpy child the next, as opposed to any long-term damage. But that's not the case with the failure to maintain that boundary. Appropriate boundaries are vital for a child's feeling of safety and security, and if he's able to 'win' a later bedtime, that makes him more powerful than you. That may be great when it comes to bedtime, but if you're not in control any more, that's terrifying to him when it comes to dealing with the big, bad world outside, because he's certainly not ready to do that on his own yet.

When your home becomes a democracy, with children having an equal say, rather than a (very benign) dictatorship, where routines and rules regarding bedtime, homework time, screen time, etc. are laid down by the parents, life becomes unpredictable and uncertain for children, and that makes them anxious. During separation and divorce, children are naturally uncertain, anxious and afraid, so they need these boundaries to be set and kept more than ever. But, of course, you probably feel less up to the task than ever. Not only that, but you're worried that your children won't like you if you make them stick to the rules, and that they might rush off into the arms of their other parent.

It's hard when you're going through the nitty gritty of divorce to keep sight of the big picture, but keep in mind that you're the parent, not your child's friend. Hopefully, your children will have many friends during the course of their lives, but you're the only mother/father they'll ever have. And your job is to help them to become an independent, mature, resilient adult.

By you being 'in charge' and setting boundaries such as insisting they help with jobs around the house, you're not being mean (although your children may be angry and shout that you are at the time), you're encouraging your children to acquire the skills they need for adult life. If you make everything easy and sort things out for them when they don't turn out as they'd have liked, you're preventing their growth. You're also setting yourself up for a very hard time as your children grow older. That said, it's important that you hold the boundaries kindly. If you're stressed, or haven't slept, you can scare your child by being too strict and that can do more damage than not keeping the boundary at all. It's important for your children that you look after yourself as well as them!

Young children are naturally self-centred, i.e. they're only interested in themselves and what's happening in their own little world. A narcissistic adult is not so endearing, and children who are allowed to think that the world revolves around them, and that they're entitled to have their needs and wishes met above those of their parents and other people, will be heading that way. By setting limits on your children's behaviour, you will interrupt this pattern and enable them to learn how to deal with frustrations and disappointments in life.

What to say and what not to say to the children

If at all possible, it's best if the two of you can tell your children together that you're splitting up, and this needs to be well planned in advance as to what you'll say. Your children will need to be reassured that, although the two of you don't want to live together any more, you both still love them as much as before. Although things are going to change, you'll both always be there for them.

You need to tell them the truth; children always know at some level when you're lying and they'll find it more difficult to trust you in the future. But you don't need to tell them the whole truth; too much information can be as hard for them as undisclosed secrets. Your divorce is adult business. You're not divorcing your children. You wouldn't talk to your children about your sex life, and they don't need to know more than the very basics of why your relationship's broken down either. The fact that you don't love each other anymore may be enough in some cases.

What your children do want to know is what's going to happen to them, and what will change in their world. You may well be at the stage where you don't yet know yourself, so tell them the truth. Explain that you're still working that bit out and that, as soon as you do know, you'll tell them. Encourage them to ask questions because you won't always be able to guess what's worrying them – things like 'will the hamster be coming too?' They will certainly be worried, confused and upset, although they'll probably do their best to hide that from you.

Parents often believe that their children are coping well with the divorce and are not adversely affected by it. Sometimes this is wishful thinking, and sometimes they're right. But, as Jane's story shows, the fact that they're not traumatised at the time doesn't mean the divorce won't have an impact later.

Jane's story

I was three, and living with my family in Cairo when my mother went off with, and eventually married, my father's best friend; she remained in Cairo. My father decided that this made her an unfit mother and, on our return to England, he sent me to live with an aunt until the divorce was settled. I was told nothing, even when I moved with my father to India with another woman he worked with, whom I eventually realised was my stepmother.

I never saw my mother again. I was 14 when she died, and I don't even recall how I found out; maybe a girl at school told me. My father adored my mother and I don't think he ever got over it; it changed him and he became very unhappy. When I was 21, my father had to tell me that I was the beneficiary of a trust fund set up by my mother, and he broke down and cried. To the end of his days, I never felt I could ask any of the things I wanted to know about my mother; as a child, there must have been some way I knew not to ask. He was a very kind man, but I knew not to upset him.

I'm 83 years old, but still dwell on the divorce and am sadder now than I ever was as a child. I have so many unanswered questions, and I've felt the absence of a mother all my life, particularly when I was bringing up my own four children, when I would have loved to have had a mother to help and advise me. (I firmly believe my mother would not have died had she remained with my father.) The divorce made me very independent, and I do believe that 'what doesn't break you makes you stronger', but maybe the biggest effect it's had on me is that I lack empathy for other people.

Listening to your children is important, although some things may be hard to hear. We don't like to see a child upset and tend to tell them it's all okay, or it's not like they think it is, in an effort to soothe them. But, in these difficult circumstances, it's important to accept and validate their painful emotions, rather than deny them and make the child wrong. Let them know it's natural that they're feeling sad/angry/confused, etc. and ask questions as to whether anything in particular has made them feel that way now, and what will make them feel better.

Although you need to let your children know that you'll be making the decisions, because you're the parents and they're the child, it's important to listen to their wishes and feelings when you're planning the future. Your children will cope better if they feel that their views have been taken into account, even if the final decision isn't actually what they wanted. It's not fair to expect them to make the decisions, and part of their security is in knowing you'll be taking care of those so they won't have to live with the consequences if they get it wrong.

Do all you can to avoid your children overhearing when you're talking on the phone or in person about your divorce. Even preverbal children will understand more than you think, and will pick up on your emotions and be worried by what they hear.

Child or play therapy

Whatever your situation, divorce is just as hard for your children to deal with as it is for you. If you're able to follow some of the suggestions in Chapter 2 for saving money on your legal fees, you may want to consider spending it instead on some professional support for your children. Play or art therapy will give them a safe and confidential space to explore any worries or questions they may have, and to have on their side someone qualified to interpret the emotions they don't have the vocabulary to express.

When your children are adults

Increasingly, older people are getting divorced. Some couples have waited until their children have grown up in order to spare them the pain of going through the divorce and assume, because the kids have moved away from home, maybe to university, that they won't be bothered. Nothing could be further from the truth. When they've lived their whole childhood believing their parents were happy together, and particularly when they're just embarking on relationships of their own, they can be shocked to the core, and believe that all those years were founded on lies.

Older adult children can also be profoundly affected, sometimes in unexpected ways. So, just because your children are fully grown, don't expect them to sail through your divorce. The same good principles outlined earlier in the chapter, such as not using your kids as an emotional crutch, are just as applicable for older children.

Christiana's story

I was an adult, in my twenties, at the time of my parents' acrimonious divorce. I was badly affected by the divorce when it happened, but it is also true that my parents had not been happy for some time. After the initial shock and betrayal, my mother has been far happier without my father and, likewise, my father largely appeared happier too. In many ways, I am glad they divorced. My own feelings of loss are subsumed by knowing that, although the circumstances were distressing, divorce was for the best.

My longer-term feelings about the divorce are mainly focused on the loss of the core parental unit and the happiness and support that provided for me. It is not the same having separate visits, conversations, holidays, etc. I coped with it, but I still missed the family unit that we were. It is hard when something that you took for granted is suddenly gone. I had 'grown up', so the situation was different, but I wonder if my feelings were similar to those of younger children.

I also regret that my children will never have seen their maternal grandparents together, so there is a lingering element of missing 'what might have been'.

But the hardest thing by far was 18 years after the divorce: my father's cancer diagnosis and consequent death 18 months later. I was distraught, but I couldn't go to my mother for comfort, or even to talk about him. Although he'd been a brilliant father to my brother and me, he'd treated my mother badly. She told me that, although she acknowledged I'd lost my father, he'd been dead to her for many years. She did say that I could talk to her about my dad, but I've never felt comfortable doing that and it just wouldn't help me, knowing that she really doesn't want to hear about him. Her attitude has made things harder for me, but I completely understand her perspective.

CHAPTER 5
DEALING WITH CUSTODY AND CO-PARENTING

Creating a parenting plan

What happens to the children should be what you, their parents, decide. The court will only become involved if you absolutely can't work it out between yourselves or in mediation. You need a parenting plan, but it doesn't need to be anything official involving a lawyer or a court.

It's best if the two of you can sit down and make a parenting plan as soon as you can. It's important that you feel as happy as you can be with your plan. Although, in theory, arrangements for children can always be changed, in practice, if children are settled in the 'wrong' home/school/country, it can be almost impossible (or at least extremely disruptive) to change later. Don't rush to agree to anything if your gut instinct tells you it's not right. Keep negotiating until you have an arrangement you can live with.

It's best if your parenting plan is in a separate document for each child; if your children are of different ages and sexes, their needs will not all be the same, although you'll be able to 'copy and paste' quite a bit of the information into each plan. You'll find examples of parenting plans online, but I also set out below some of the main things to consider. Your plan should cover more than just where the children will live and how often they'll see the other parent, although those are obviously the first crucial decisions to be made.

Other things you may want to have in your plan include:

- How/where/who will transport the children between their parents?
- When with one parent, how, and how often, will the children communicate with their other parent?
- If a parent is not going to be available to have the children when expected, how and when will this be negotiated with the other

parent, and how will the change be explained to the children?

- Which clothes, toys, bikes, computers, etc. stay at each parent's house and which need to be moved each time?
- With which parent will the children spend their birthdays? Will the children have birthday parties and, if so, which parent will organise/pay for these? Will the other parent attend?
- Where will the children be on their parents' birthdays? And what about Mother's Day and Father's Day?
- What time will the children have with each parent at Christmas?
- How much time will each parent have with the children in school holidays?
- Do both parents agree the other can take the children abroad? If so, for how long? How much notice needs to be given to the other parent? Which parent is responsible for obtaining/paying for/keeping the children's passports?
- If both parents are working, what childcare arrangements are to be made?
- Which schools will the children attend? Will both parents be able to visit/choose new schools together if/when a child needs to change school?
- Will both parents attend parents' evenings, school concerts, etc.? If so, will they go separately or together?
- Does the school need to be asked to provide reports and all other information to both parents or will one be responsible for telling the other?
- Which out-of-school activities will each child be involved in? Which parent will take them and how will the costs be met?
- What time is bedtime on school days and at weekends?
- Are any strategies necessary for managing behaviour?
- How is homework to be managed?
- What mobile phones, etc. will each child have and which parent is responsible for providing/replacing these?

- What limits are there on screen time?

- What happens if a child is unwell? Do they still go to the other parent? Which parent is responsible for any medical/dental appointments? Is the other parent to be informed and, if so, how and when?

- Does a child need a special diet? Are the parents agreed on anything the child should not eat?

- What happens if one of the parents is ill or incapacitated? Do the children go to the other parent, other family members or would childcare be needed? What about if one parent were to die?

- How soon will children be introduced to a new partner of either parent?

- How will they be prepared for this?

- How will the parents communicate with each other?

- When will the parenting plan be reviewed? How often you review your plan(s) will depend on the ages of your children, their needs and your particular circumstances.

Once you've completed your plan(s), it should be signed by both parents, who should each keep a copy.

Deciding whether shared care/joint custody is appropriate

Please note that the terms 'custody' and 'access' have often been used in this book, because that's how most people still refer to them. In fact, they were changed to 'residence' and 'contact' in the Children Act 1989, and more recently to a 'Child Arrangements Programme (CAP)', which are the terms you'll hear if you do go to court.

Shared care is becoming more common, mainly I suspect because it's felt to be fairer for the parents to be able to have equal time with their children. But is it fair to the children? How often do they have to move between homes? How far is it, and how difficult is it for them?

Constantly moving between two homes is a lot to ask of a child, and some will cope better than others. A boy on the ADD/autistic spectrum, for instance, will find any change difficult and really struggle with such an arrangement, whereas his big sister may thrive on the regular time with both parents, and become a super-organised adult in time. A lot will depend on how the parents handle the situation, too. If they have an easy relationship and are able to talk through any issues as they arise, the children may settle well into the arrangement and benefit from the very short gaps between times with each parent.

But if the parents are at loggerheads, or one feels they are walking on eggshells around the other, each move to the other home is going to be emotionally fraught for the children, who may suffer stress, depression or other long-term consequences. Shared care is not appropriate in these circumstances.

Cheryl and Sam's story

When Cheryl and Sam split up, he went to live in a converted unit that was part of her parents' bed and breakfast accommodation in the Lake District, just a mile from the family home. This was a perfect arrangement for them to share the care of Hugo, aged seven, and Anna, aged six, as the kids had been used to spending a lot of time at their grandparents'. Although Cheryl was disillusioned with Sam as a husband (to put it kindly!), she was still able to respect him as an excellent hands-on father to their children. She knew he would care for them well, although she was also reassured knowing that her parents were on hand if there should ever be a problem.

Most families are not going to have such an ideal solution as Cheryl and Sam, but shared care works best when parents live as close to each other as possible, and as close to the school as they can. It can also be easier for children if they're collected from school by the other parent, rather than having to say goodbye to the parent they're with.

What works for a child when they're six may no longer suit them when they're 12, so it's important to keep listening to your children's wishes and feelings, and adapt your arrangements as and when necessary.

Communicating successfully with your ex

When your relationship breaks down, communication often breaks down too. If you want to minimise the damage to your children, you may need to find a different way to deal with your ex, as it's essential for your children's wellbeing that you do continue to communicate about them. If conversation tends to deteriorate into an argument, use email or texts instead, but don't be tempted to make the mistake of replying instantly, unless it's an emergency. Most things can wait 12 or 24 hours for a reply and, wherever possible, it's best to sleep on it. Ask yourself 'what's in my child's best interests here?' before deciding what to write.

Another question to ask yourself before sending an angry or abusive message, or posting your venom on social media, is this: 'would I feel okay if this message ends up being read by a judge in court?' Although that's not likely, it's always a possibility, and thinking from this viewpoint can be really helpful in lowering the temperature. If you wouldn't be comfortable with others knowing what you've said, and if it would harm your case if it did end up in court, it's best not to say it.

If you really can't communicate with your ex, you can have a notebook which is passed between you, along with any belongings for your child, on access handovers. You can write short notes to each other about your children such as 'Annie needs to do 10 minutes' reading each day: book in bag' or 'Ben has been prescribed antibiotics for his chest infection, please give four times a day, next one due at 4pm.'

You need to accept that your ex is going to push your buttons: it goes with the territory. Here's a simple technique you can try to help cope with this.

- How often are you provoked by your ex?
- In what circumstances?
- How quickly do you become aware that it's happened?
- How do you react?

The instant you become aware that your ex has said or done something you don't like, and before you say or do anything in response, say to yourself 'I am responsible'.

This doesn't mean you're responsible for the dreadful thing that your ex has just done or said. It means that you're responsible for the way you react to it, and, as a responsible parent, you're responsible for not making a bad situation worse and for limiting the damage to your children. Taking this responsibility stops you being a victim and empowers you to choose the best way forward, for yourself and your children.

Having said to yourself 'I'm responsible', you may need to say to your ex, 'I need to think about that and I'll get back to you'. When you start reacting differently to your ex, they'll start behaving differently towards you.

Tackling custody threats

Separation and divorce are traumatic and sometimes dramatic times, which can plunge people into dark, ugly places. They can experience intense emotions, which they're unused to and unable to control, and they can say some awful things. Of course, the person hearing those things is also in this same dark place and often unable to work out which of the insults are meaningless and which they need to take seriously. They can be paralysed by a threat about their children – which, if they were able to think straight they would see was an empty one – and they're left unable to move forward.

If your partner makes a threat, don't let it keep going round and round in your head. Sit down with someone you trust and pick it to pieces to see if there's any substance to it at all.

'I'll get custody of the children because you're a bad mother'

This cuts any mother to the quick, as of course it's designed to. And the mother who's in the process of separating will already have lost a lot of her confidence as a result of the situation, so a threat like this can be enough to stop her leaving, which is often the aim.

Let's look at the 'bad mother' bit first. The real question is this: are you a 'good enough' mother, or have you caused, or put your children at risk of, significant harm? If you had harmed your children, why would their father wait until now to mention it? Has he been going out to work and leaving the children with you all day? If so, he can't be that worried, or you can't have done anything that terrible. So, it's usually best to treat these threats with the contempt they deserve. Take the moral high ground and say nothing.

If your partner's behaviour towards you has caused you to become so confused that you still can't decide whether you're a good enough mother, see Chapter 8, which deals with personality disorders and other mental health issues.

The court won't make any orders about your children unless one of you asks it to. So, when he says he'll get custody, is he really going to make an application to the court? The court fee is £215 at the time of writing, and a solicitor's fee for making the application will be five or 10 times more than that. And, before you can make an application to the court, you have to attend a Mediation Information Assessment Meeting (MIAM) with a mediator. The idea behind this is to resolve your issues in mediation rather than in court, if at all possible.

If your partner did take you to court, what would be his chances of success? If you're the one working full time and he's been at home looking after the children, then he's got a very good chance of getting custody. Not because you're a bad mother, but because he's the one who's been doing that job and is available to do it, whereas you're not. Of course, the opposite is equally true if he's been the one working full time.

Shared custody is becoming more common these days. The question that needs to be asked is always 'what's best for my children?' And if you have more than one, they each need to be considered in turn, as what works for one will not necessarily work for another. The court will only make an order in respect of children if it's better than making no order, and the judge will always do what they consider to be in the best interests of the children.

If you have teenage boys, they may well want to live with their father. It's not uncommon for boys who've lived perfectly happily for many years with their mother to decide they want to live with their father when they're older. It's nothing to do with you being a bad mother, or with you at all really, it's just they need that male role model at that time in their lives.

'You won't see your children again'

This, sadly, is a threat much more likely to be fulfilled than the last one. More than one in three children lose contact with a parent (usually their father) after divorce. It's hard for parents not to see their children every day. Some simply can't cope with the pain of seeing their children for a short while and then not seeing them for a long time, and opt out. Others just opt out straight away. And some have so many problems of their own (such as alcoholism), they just can't deal with access arrangements. Others are prevented by the other parent from having any proper contact with their children, even when several applications to the court are made.

Whatever the reason, it's usually a huge loss for the child. Even if their parent is a 'waste of space', a child needs to be allowed to come to that conclusion for themselves, rather than forever feel deprived of the love of a parent they increasingly idealise in their minds.

If you're threatened with not seeing your children again, you should perhaps count yourself lucky: you have been warned! Others find it's crept up on them slowly and insidiously and they may not realise until it's too late. This is a threat that needs to be nipped in the bud. If your ex is being difficult over contact, it's time for an honest conversation with yourself. Have you really been a hands-on parent at every opportunity or have you been distracted by work or other matters? Could there be a genuine concern for the children's wellbeing while they're with you? Whether or not there could be a reason, a good question to ask your ex is: 'what do I need to do to be able to see the children?' And then you may need to swallow your pride, and do whatever is asked of you while you're resolving the issue. If supervised contact is requested, do it, however unnecessary you consider it to be. You must take every opportunity to see your children, and never miss a visit or you're in danger of your contact being further reduced rather than increased.

If the answer to your question is simply an angry retort that you're not going to see your children, don't be tempted to reply in anger. You need to model the best behaviour you can muster at all times with your ex. Don't give them any ammunition to weaken your case. Don't waste any time, either; is there a family member or friend who can help you to reach agreement with your ex? If not, find a mediator who will write to your ex and invite them to join you for a meeting. If they don't respond, you could get a solicitor to write a letter to them. This can often be regarded as an aggressive step, so make sure it's a friendly and constructive letter and that you see and approve it before it's sent.

If all else fails, you'll need to apply to the court for a child arrangements order so that your ex can be ordered to make your children available to see you.

CHAPTER 6
DEALING WITH MONEY, PROPERTY AND PENSIONS

What to do about the house

Divorce is a scary time, and people make threats in the heat of the moment that won't or can't be carried out but are still frightening to hear. And there's nothing much scarier than feeling you're going to be left without a home. But, children aren't left homeless in this country and people's worst fears rarely come true. You need to have a plan for your divorce, as set out in Chapter 1, and you don't leave one home until you know where the next one is. Yes, you may have to downsize, but don't be pressured into agreeing to put your house on the market until you know how much of the net proceeds of the sale you'll be receiving, and how your next home is going to be funded.

Whichever process you use to arrive at your financial settlement (see Chapter 1), the factors to be taken into account are the same. The starting point for dividing up a couple's assets is a 50/50 split but, unless the couple have no children, earn very similar amounts, and have contributed the same to their home and/or other assets, it's not the finishing point in English law. If you're worried about being left homeless, your case will almost certainly be decided on need alone. If you have children, you should get enough to re-house yourself and your children, at least until they're 18.

Building a financial plan for life after divorce

You may fear that you can't afford to divorce because there's not enough money to live on. But don't just assume this is the case without taking some advice, particularly if you're a mother with children at home.

The Citizens Advice Bureau (CAB) will be able to advise you of any additional state benefits you'd be entitled to, and the court (if it comes to that) will always ensure that any children are housed and fed. If you need to leave a bad relationship, there's always a way. You'll have to do the research necessary to find it, and ask for help where you need it, and sometimes hard choices are involved, but it's always possible.

Some CABs have free legal advice sessions, and many solicitors offer a free half-hour's advice. Make the most of all the free advice you can get by preparing well (see Chapter 2), so you're clear about what you've got and what you need.

When there's a young family involved, and a wife has given up her career prospects to bring up the children, she's likely to get a larger percentage of the matrimonial assets. This results in bitterness and resentment in a lot of husbands who feel they've lost everything and yet still have to keep paying for their wife and children for several years. Whilst it can indeed be hard for a husband initially, if they're progressing up a career ladder, their salary is likely to keep increasing over the years, whereas his ex-wife is likely to remain on a low salary. It is ex-wives, rather than husbands, who can end up in poverty in the long term.

It's very important, therefore, that, before agreeing to their divorce settlement, any wife (unless they're very young) should get a cash flow forecast from a financial advisor to show how much they're likely to have to live on in later life.

Once you have a full picture of your needs, you'll be in a good position to start negotiating your financial settlement and the division of your assets.

Completing the dreaded Form E

If you're using a solicitor, or going to court, you'll have to complete this 28-page financial form that provides a detailed picture of your finances. If you're going to a mediator, they're likely to have their own form, which, hopefully, will be less onerous. Solicitors will generally give little advice before they have a Form E from both you and your spouse, so it's best, if possible, to do these first and save yourself money in fees.

Form E generally takes clients between one and three months to complete – sometimes much longer as the task is so daunting. It's best to break it down into small chunks and not try to do it all at once. However, you do need to go through it all first and prioritise any information you need to obtain from other sources, as some things may take time to gather. For example, you'll be required to produce valuations of your pension(s) (see later in the chapter) and these can take many weeks to arrive, so this should be your first task. You may also need mortgage statements, business accounts or other documents. The next thing to do is to start your list of outgoings as you won't remember them all at once, particularly things that only happen once a year. It may help to carry a little notebook around with you so you can jot down everything you spend, or you can make space for this in your divorce notebook/journal. It's no good agreeing a figure for maintenance and then discovering a few months later that you can't manage on that amount.

Be sure to state that any valuations or estimates of your future needs are provisional; negotiations and/or court proceedings can take a long time and a lot can change before a final settlement!

Most of Form E is clear, but some bits are not so obvious and, if your financial affairs are in any way complicated, you may need help with the form. Your solicitor will, of course, help you with it, but, as it's a financial form, consider whether your accountant or financial advisor would be a better (and cheaper) person to help. If there's any possibility of your divorce having any tax implications (and this could apply even to the family home), an accountant may be a better person to advise you. You can get your accountant or solicitor to help (not only is an accountant likely to be cheaper, they'll be more knowledgeable on your finances), or you can look online. The Advice Now website (www.advicenow.org.uk) has an easy-to-understand download giving sample answers, and there's lots of information on Wikivorce (www.wikivorce.com), including a help sheet that should answer most questions.

Form E includes questions about pensions. Solicitors are not experts on pensions and they will ask a pension expert to prepare a report on your pension, and/or your spouse's pension, if it's of any significant value. You may be able to get this yourself, without paying a solicitor several units of their time to get one for you. Not all accountants or financial advisors are pension experts, so you'll need to find one who is.

Form E is an important document and you must consider carefully what you say as it may come back to haunt you. For example, if you say 'our house should be sold and the proceeds divided in a particular way', and then later realise your children need to stay in their own home and you want to argue for the house to be transferred to you, it will be much more difficult.

What's the difference between a consent order and a clean break order?

These two orders are completely different animals, serving entirely different functions but can be confusing. A consent order is a financial settlement agreed between you and your spouse which is made legally binding in a court order, prepared for you by a solicitor.

A clean break order, on the other hand, ends all financial ties between you and your spouse so that neither of you can go back to court later, no matter what happens in the future.

A clean break may be included in a consent order, or it may be declared by a judge after a court hearing if the couple can't agree.

However, if one ex-spouse is to continue paying maintenance to the other, then it's not a clean break. In this situation, the ongoing maintenance is either set out in a consent order (assuming both parties have agreed), or it may be part of a financial order made by a judge (in cases where the parties can't reach agreement between themselves). There's more on this, and child maintenance, later.

Understanding the clean break order

The divorce itself, i.e. your decree absolute, ends your marriage contract and enables you to remarry. Full stop. That's it, nothing else.

It says nothing about the financial ties and obligations between you. Unless you also have a clean break order from the court, your financial claims remain open, and either of you could take the other to court at any time – and even after the death of one of you.

If that's not what you want, a clean break order puts an end to all the financial claims either of you may have against the other, forever. It means that your assets have been divided and no more maintenance will be paid (for a spouse. You can't have a clean break from your children). The court always favours a clean break order, so long as it's fair to both parties to make one.

But, if ongoing maintenance is to be paid to a spouse (most often to a wife, until she can go back to work if she's caring for young children, or for the rest of her life if she's older and unlikely to be able to work again or earn enough), it's still possible to have a capital clean break.

A capital clean break means that your assets have been divided and neither of you can go back to court about property or other financial assets. If a maintenance order is made, it's always possible to go back to court to have it varied, and there's still a financial tie, so it's not a full clean break.

Do you need a clean break order?

You may remember hearing about Dale Vince's rags to riches story in 2015 when his ex-wife, Kathleen Wyatt, made a claim for £1.9m of the estimated £57m fortune made from his Ecotricity business, over 30 years after they separated. When he left her, Mr Vince became a New Age traveller and, when they eventually divorced in 1992, he did not pay maintenance for either his ex-wife or their children because he had no money, and they had no property or savings to divide.

Mr Vince tried to argue that he had obtained a clean break order in 1992 but he was unable to produce a copy of the document, and the court had lost the file.

Like Dale Vince, you may think you've little or no money or assets now and so you have no need for an order (which I suspect is what happened with Ms Wyatt and Mr Vince). But, ask yourself this: if in two or 10 years' time you were to win £1m on the lottery, or inherit a large sum of money, would you gladly give up to half to your ex? If your answer is 'yes', then you probably don't need a clean break order. If your ex were to have a bad accident and be unable to work again, would you be happy to pay her/him maintenance for the rest of their life? If your answer is 'no', then a clean break order would be a wise insurance policy. If you have no assets or income to divide, you can just have a very simple clean break order, which will be quick, cheap and easy to obtain. You may be able to get this done for a fixed fee of as little as £60 plus VAT, probably less than your annual travel insurance premium.

In the end, Mr Vince was only ordered to pay his ex-wife £300,000 – a small sum to him (although he also had to pay her legal fees, which were more than that, as well as his own), but he described the decision as 'mad'. I'm sure it seems that way to those who don't understand the law and assume that divorce ends all financial claims. Perhaps it does in other places, but in England and Wales, you also need to have a clean break order as well as your decree absolute to fully dissolve your ties.

Usually, the clean break clauses are just part of the whole financial agreement which a solicitor puts into a consent order.

Understanding the consent order

When you and your spouse have reached agreement about your property, pensions, savings and other assets, one of you needs to ask a solicitor to put this into a formal legal document. If you both have a solicitor, the other solicitor will need to approve the document, or ask for any amendments to be made.

Once it's finalised, both of you have to sign this draft order and it's then sent to the court, together with a form setting out your basic financial situation; again, you both have to complete and sign this to say you've seen the other party's information.

Remember that your consent order can have a clean break clause written in, ensuring the financial ties between you and your spouse are permanently cut.

A judge will consider the agreement and decide whether it's fair to both parties. So, unlike the actual divorce proceedings, it's not just a rubber-stamp exercise. The solicitor drawing up your agreement should advise you as to the likelihood of it being approved by the judge, and they won't want to send in one that isn't likely to be approved. So, usually, the order will be approved by the judge, drawn up on court paper, and returned to the solicitor (if that's who sent it in).

Only on rare occasions would you have to go to court, for example, if the judge is not happy with your proposed order for some reason and wants to ask you a few questions.

When you receive your final order, make sure you keep it safe – along with your decree absolute and your birth certificate, etc. These are vital documents and courts have been known to lose files, as they did with Dale Vince's, in which case, you can't get a duplicate. And if your ex were to make a claim against you in 30 years' time, you'd be very relieved to be able to flourish this document at them!

Is spousal maintenance included in your consent order?

It can be, yes, or it can be decided by a court order in cases where couples don't agree.

When one spouse is to continue to pay maintenance to the other, there are a few different options for getting this on paper. A maintenance order (also known as a periodical payments order), can either be for a fixed period of time that's perhaps as short as a few months or years, while the recipient works towards financial independence (by retraining or getting back into the workplace, for instance). Or it could last much longer, such as until the youngest child finishes university education, or until retirement. A maintenance order that ends on the expiry of a fixed term is effectively a deferred clean break.

If spousal maintenance is ordered on an open-ended basis (known as a joint lives order), it lasts until either party dies, or the person receiving the regular payments remarries, or there is a successful application to end it.

A third option is a 'nominal' maintenance order (e.g. 5p per year). This means that no actual money changes hands, but there's no clean break either (and the nominal order can be for joint lives or for a fixed term). The purpose of a nominal maintenance order is to act as a safety net for the potential recipient, in case he or she needs to ask for substantive financial help from the other party in the future.

Is child maintenance included in your consent order?

The court is not usually able to make orders for child maintenance. In cases where couples can't agree child maintenance between themselves, this is now dealt with by the Child Maintenance Service (CMS), the government service that replaced the Child Support Agency (CSA) in 2013. The ins and outs of child maintenance is beyond the scope of this book, however, my general advice about going down the CMS route is the same as about going to court: avoid it if you possibly can. Some solicitors may be able to give you some advice about the CMS but, as it's not something they typically deal with, many of them will not be able to help you much either.

If you both want what's best for your children, you should be able to negotiate (whether over the kitchen table or through mediation or solicitors) the right amount to be paid to meet the needs of your children and avoid paying the hefty fees of the CMS. However, they do have a useful, and free, calculator on their website, which may give you some guidance as to an appropriate amount. Once you've agreed a figure, you could record it in your parenting plan (see Chapter 5) if you need a written record, but the amount to be paid will need to be varied over the years as the children's needs change and the cost of living increases.

Although the court can't make maintenance orders for children when parents don't agree, maintenance can be included in a consent order, usually in the preamble (agreed clauses before the actual order). There may also be an agreement in the order that the receiving parent agrees not to apply to the CMS as long as the paying parent pays £X per month (often with provision for increases).

Are school and university fees included in your consent order?

They should be, yes. Parents can also agree to a provision in their court order that each of them pay into a fund for school fees, school trips, or university education.

Ignore pensions at your peril

Pensions are often the biggest asset in the marriage after the marital home, and will need to be considered as part of your financial agreement. You will usually have to obtain the Cash Equivalent Transfer Value (CETV) of your pension from your provider, who may make a charge for this, and it may take a few months. Pensions are complicated and you may need financial advice, or a valuation of the pension by an actuary.

Pensions may be dealt with in one of three ways:

- Pension sharing – where the pension is split at the time of divorce so that the other person receives a separate pension to invest elsewhere and can continue to build pension benefits for the future.

- Pension offsetting – where you each keep your own pension funds but adjust the proportion of other assets, such as the house, to take account of the value of the pension benefits.

- Pension earmarking – where, when the pension holder starts to draw their pension, part of the payments will be paid to their ex.

Tackling financial threats

When faced with the prospect of divorce, some spouses lash out with financial threats. Let's explore some of the most common threats that my clients have faced.

'I'll leave you homeless and/or penniless'

This is sometimes said by an angry husband to his wife who is wanting to leave. Although it's scary to hear, it's an empty threat. Everyone who is married has the protection of the law and no one will be left either homeless or penniless by the court. If there are children and the wife is only working part time, if at all, she is likely to get the greater share of the assets. Remember, your spouse may feel threatened themselves, making them lash out. So, if they say this to you, a little compassion (rather than an angry retort) may serve you better than a pointless argument.

If an angry spouse can't be persuaded from this position, the other party will have no option but to issue a divorce petition and then apply to the court for a financial remedy. Before you can make an application, you'll need to attend a Mediation Information and Assessment Meeting (MIAM) to see if your differences can be resolved through mediation rather than going to court.

'I won't pay for the children'

This is usually said in the heat of the moment. Most parents are willing to pay maintenance for their children, so, again, it's a threat not to be taken too seriously.

If, however, your ex does prove to be serious about this, you'll have to apply to the CMS for help. If you need advice on this issue, the CAB is likely to know more about it than a solicitor.

'I'll hide what I've got'

In a divorce, the division of assets takes place after full financial disclosure by both parties. This means that absolutely every item you own that is worth more than £500 has to be listed, and properties, businesses and pensions have to be valued. These details are shared with your spouse, and vice versa.

Even in this day and age, some couples are not aware of how much each other has. Others may know, or suspect, there are other hidden funds (for instance, in off-shore accounts) but may not be able to prove it. One lady told me her husband had a large suitcase full of bank notes hidden in his brother's house; she was certainly going to have a hard job proving that.

If you're going to use mediation or collaborative law to reach your financial settlement, this depends upon both parties being totally open and honest about their income and assets. If they're not, then court proceedings have to be issued so that the court can be asked to make an order for full disclosure. Of course, this is expensive and will cost you several thousands of pounds, so you have to be sure that the undisclosed assets are worth more – or that the principle is worth that outlay to you.

In the past, it's often not been worth this huge expense for wives (usually) who've not known or been able to prove what was at stake, and the courts weren't always too helpful in such cases. All that changed in October 2015, however, when two wealthy wives took their cases all the way to the Supreme Court. They had both received less in their divorce settlements than they would have done if their husbands had fully disclosed their assets. The court overturned their original settlements, making it clear that dishonesty would not be tolerated and setting an unambiguous precedent for the future. These husbands not only had to pay their wives what they were entitled to in the first place, they also had to pay for a second court hearing to determine this, as well as all the appeal hearings to have the first order revoked. They had to pay their own legal costs as well as those of their wives – who didn't go to the cheapest solicitors in London.

These two wives have done a huge service to less wealthy wives who would never have been able to afford these appeals. So, whilst I normally recommend treating divorce threats with the contempt they deserve and trying to keep the peace by not retaliating, if you're on the receiving end of one like this, you can respond with a threat (or rather a promise) of your own: that you'll leave no stone unturned until you find what they've hidden, however long that may take, and that you'll take them back to court, however much that may cost them.

'I'll give the judge copies of your documents'

The bad news here is going to seem a bit of a contradiction after the good news above, but you're not allowed to take your spouse's documents and show them to the judge. The Court of Appeal decided this in 2010 in a ridiculous case that's been labelled the 'cheat's charter'. Prior to that, it was okay to take documents belonging to the other party, provided they were copied and given straight back.

Now, it depends on whether the documents are considered confidential. If bank statements are left on the kitchen table, they wouldn't be, whereas if they were in the owner's study or briefcase, they would be.

A solicitor will no longer touch any document belonging to their client's spouse as they could be prosecuted for this, and so could you. Don't do it! If you've seen documents relating to assets which are not disclosed by your spouse at the appropriate time, you'll have to rely on your memory to be able to question this.

'I'll give up my job so you won't get any money'

I'm afraid this does happen, although it's a threat more often made than carried out. If you know that your spouse's job/career is important to them, you'll not take this one too seriously, especially if they've been in a good position for some time.

However, if you think the threat might be serious, make sure that you make a note of the date(s) the threat was made, exactly what was said and the circumstances. Or you could pick up your phone and ask them to repeat what they just said so you can record it. This means that, if they were to give up their job, but then say in court they were made redundant or sacked, you have evidence to the contrary. It won't go down well with the judge and you're likely to get more of the assets to make up for it.

Busting common divorce myths

There are also a number of myths floating around the area of money and financial settlements. Here I debunk some of the more common myths.

'When we divorce, my ex won't be entitled to any of the money I've made since we separated several years ago'

Your financial position is considered as at the time of your application for a financial remedy (settlement). What's happened since the separation can be taken into account, and if the other party needs more, they'll get it. This may feel unjust to a party who has done well since their separation, so it's a reason not to delay your divorce too long.

'My spouse has been unfaithful so I'll get a bigger financial settlement'

The divorce proceedings, i.e. whatever happened in the marriage, are different and separate from the financial remedy (see Chapter 7), and therefore don't have any effect on the financial settlement. The exception to this is financial misconduct; the court can and does make adjustments in the financial order if there's been financial misconduct, even if it's not done with the object of diminishing the other person's claim. Even if you've enjoyed a high standard of living during the marriage, avoid having expensive holidays or meals out if your spouse is struggling to meet their household expenditure. Now is not the time for either party to be using joint or personal savings to invest in business deals or even to help out friends or relatives with gifts or loans. Ideally, both parties should agree on an interim budget, with clarity as to how it will be met, until finances are finalised.

People often try to fight for more, feeling they're justified because of what happened in the marriage, but there's no legal basis for it. On the other hand, people who've been unfaithful sometimes feel so guilty they're willing to give more to the other party than they'd be legally obliged to.

'I'll lose too much because it was me who had an affair'

People often feel that they will (or maybe that they should) be punished for any wrong-doing within the marriage, but this doesn't happen in English divorce law unless they've done something that amounts to a criminal offence. A couple's money and assets are divided according to need and other factors laid down by law, none of which include behaviour in the marriage (apart from financial misconduct, see above).

When it comes to arrangements for your kids, the time each parent spends with the children should be determined mostly in accordance with the needs of the children, and certainly not by the need to 'punish' one of their parents.

'We never married, but we've lived together for 20 years, and have three children. This means I'm a common-law wife and I'll get the same as if we were married'

Six out of every 10 couples who live together believe that they have the same protection as married couples if they split up. They don't. The myth of common-law marriage and the fact that many official bodies refer to people 'living together as husband and wife' means that many people who live together are not aware that they have no rights when their relationships end. Most of the legal information in this book will not apply to you if you're not married.

'We've divided everything fairly between us so we don't need a court order'

The case of Mr Vince, the wind farm man, was an unusual one because of the length of time after the divorce, and the amount of money he had made since. Divorces of less wealthy people rarely make the news, but if your ex were to make a claim against you in three or five years' time, how would you cope with that? Even if you 'know' they wouldn't do that, can you be equally sure that any future partner they may have wouldn't be able to persuade them to pursue you? However amicable your agreement, it really is worth getting a court order now, as a one-off insurance policy that ties up all the loose ends. You can then both move forward with certainty.

CHAPTER 7
DEALING WITH
THE DIVORCE PETITION

How to apply for a divorce

To be eligible to apply for divorce, you need to have been married for at least a year, and you have to show that your marriage has broken down with no chance of you getting back together again. This is demonstrated either by you having been separated for two years, or by citing adultery or unreasonable behaviour (see below).

There's no need to pay a solicitor to do your divorce petition for you. You can complete and submit the divorce petition yourself. The difference between doing it yourself and instructing a solicitor is this: the solicitor will send your petition and other forms to the court, and the court will send all documents back to the solicitor, rather than direct to you. Your solicitor will then forward the documents to you, hopefully with any necessary explanations.

The petitioner (applicant), or their solicitor, sends two copies of the divorce petition to the court. The court then gives the petition a case number (which you must be sure to put on all future forms and any letters you send to the court), keeps one copy and sends one copy to the other party (the respondent) with a form: the acknowledgement of service. The respondent has to complete the acknowledgement of service to confirm they have received the papers and say whether they agree or disagree with the divorce.

The court won't proceed with the divorce until it knows the respondent has received the petition and knows about the divorce.

What you need to prove for a divorce

Grounds for a no-fault divorce are:

1. You've been separated for two years **and** your spouse agrees to the divorce.

2. You've been separated for five years.

Grounds for a fault-based divorce are:

1. Adultery – where your spouse has committed adultery (which, in the eyes of the law, means they have had sex with a person of the opposite sex) and you find it intolerable to live with them. Note that many marriages do continue after an affair, so, if you've lived with your spouse for more than six months after you found out about the adultery, the court won't grant your divorce as the delay means, in the eyes of the law, that you were willing to disregard the adultery.

2. Unreasonable behaviour – where your spouse has behaved in such an unreasonable way that you can't bear to live with them.

You can see from these four grounds that, if you want a 'civilised' divorce, which is not based on blaming the bad behaviour of the other person, you're likely to have to wait two years for it. This may not be a problem, though. It often takes that long to reorganise the life of a family and to come to a final financial agreement.

But your financial agreement is not final until it's been made into a financial order (consent order) sent by a solicitor to the court. And, as explained in Chapter 1, the court can't grant (approve) a final financial order until you have a decree nisi. There are certain circumstances in which you need the certainty of a final financial order sooner rather than later, for instance, if you're taking on a new mortgage. So, you may have no option but for one of you to apply for divorce on the basis of the unreasonable behaviour of the other, to save having to wait two years. But 'unreasonable behaviour' is not as dramatic as it sounds, once you understand the process.

Behaviour petitions: How unreasonable is unreasonable?

Actually, the behaviour doesn't have to be that unreasonable at all; it's simply a case of the behaviour of one spouse being unacceptable to the other. At the end of the day, we're all human, and we're all unreasonable at times, though what's unreasonable to you may not be to me. One wife may feel lonely and neglected because her husband works long hours, while another may be delighted that hers provides so well for her growing shoe collection! It's the same behaviour, but the first wife has a ground for divorce, and the second one doesn't. It's all about perspective. If you've both agreed to a divorce on a behaviour basis, the details of that behaviour can be pretty mild and, ideally, you would agree them between you before filing. You only need three or four examples of such behaviour – just enough to show that you can't live together any more. Judges will not query what you put as long as there's some element of behaviour, even if it's trivial or vague. But don't be tempted just to say that you don't get on any more – that's not behaviour, and it won't be accepted. If it's your petition and you feel you've also behaved badly, you can acknowledge that, but you still need to put in some of your spouse's behaviour too.

If, however, you have to issue a divorce petition without the agreement of your spouse, you may need to make some stronger points. Either way, the petition should be shown to your spouse before it's sent to the court; every effort should be made wherever possible to agree on the contents of the petition. Your spouse may want something changed that you're happy to agree to, which enables them to agree to the divorce going through. This will save you both a lot of time and money.

If you do receive a behaviour petition you haven't agreed, and which incenses you, try to agree a 'watered down' version of it, rather than being tempted to issue a cross-petition or defend the divorce. Most things are negotiable in divorce!

Also bear in mind that no one else need ever know what's in your petition unless you choose to tell them. I'd suggest you don't transfer the petition online or by email as you can never know where it might end up and who else could see it. Instead, just fill it in on-screen, print out the copies you need and then delete it. But do make sure you keep a copy for yourself (as well as the two you need to send to the court) as you'll need to refer back to it later. Your decree absolute will not refer to the grounds of your divorce, so you can both rest assured that the grounds will remain private. Ultimately, it really doesn't matter what you say as long as it gets you your divorce. Divorcing on the grounds of 'unreasonable behaviour' is not pleasant, and hopefully the law will be changed soon to make it easier for couples. You just have to see the offending words as a means to an end, and remember that they'll do you no harm.

Whatever is said in your divorce petition has no effect on children or financial matters

As stated in Chapter 1, these are all separate proceedings. People worry that what is said about their behaviour in the divorce petition will count against them if there's an application in relation to their children, or for financial or property matters. And other people hope that their spouse will be punished during such proceedings for what they've done. This is absolutely not the case at all. It may have been true in the distant past but, in 2017, behaviour will only be considered in extreme cases, such as where one party's behaviour has caused such harm to the other that they can't work again, or in cases of financial misconduct, where they have depleted the family assets.

If there are children or financial proceedings, the behaviour cited in the divorce petition would have to be repeated in those other proceedings for the court to take any notice of it. If you were to go down this route, remember that your spouse would then have a chance to put across their side of it, too. (They can't do that in the divorce proceedings, because what's said there simply isn't important enough – in terms of the divorce itself, unreasonable behaviour is just a means to an end.)

What if I don't understand the forms and get something wrong?

The number of divorce petitions rejected by the court for errors is huge – about 40%, I believe. And that, of course, includes petitions sent in by solicitors. If you've made a mistake yourself, the court will simply send it back to you to amend and return it to them, so it will cost you the price of another stamp. (Unless, of course, you have another wedding booked, in which case, the delay could be very costly!)

Please note that I'm talking only about the divorce paperwork itself here. A divorce is a purely procedural matter and you will get your decree absolute when the process has been completed correctly. It's much more important if you're dealing with proceedings relating to a child, or to a financial remedy, to get your paperwork right first time. Otherwise, it can reflect very badly on you and damage your case if it appears you're trying to mislead your spouse or the court. However, details related to your children and financial situation are more likely to be well within your own knowledge, so you're less likely to get something wrong than on a divorce petition, which is all about legal procedure.

How much does it cost to divorce, and who pays?

Here we're talking only about the cost of the actual divorce, from the petition to the decree absolute, which does not include any financial order or any proceedings relating to children.

There is a court fee which, at the time of writing, is £550. (If you're on benefits or unable to afford this, you may be able to ask the court for an exemption.) If you're going to do all the divorce paperwork yourself, it'll cost you just the £550 and your postage. However, if you ask a solicitor to do your divorce for you, or use an online service, the court fee is always payable in addition to their fees.

A solicitor will charge between £200 and £2,000 to do your divorce. Online services vary and you need to be sure you understand exactly what you're getting for your money. Is it just the divorce petition itself? Remember, the divorce does not end the financial ties between you and your spouse. Some online services include the drafting of a financial consent order too, but you need to be more careful with that. Will it be drafted by a solicitor and what insurance do they have if things go wrong? What help will they give you if the court rejects your application?

I give my clients the help and advice they need to do the divorce paperwork themselves, and charge between £20 and £120 for this service. Alternatively, you can go to www.dealingwithdivorce.co.uk for a simple step-by-step guide to doing it all yourself.

At the end of the divorce petition, there's a section still quaintly called a 'prayer'. This gives you an opportunity to ask the court to order the other party to pay your costs, i.e. the court fee and any solicitor's or online fees for the divorce (but not for any children or financial proceedings which may follow). If you're happy to pay the costs yourself, don't tick that box.

People who divorce on the ground of two years' separation often split the fees between them, so you can insert the word 'half' before the word 'costs' in the prayer section if you like. But, if it's all amicable, you don't really need the court to order your spouse to pay half. You can just sort it out between you.

If the petition is a fault-based petition, it's common, but certainly not essential, to ask for an order for the other party to pay all the costs. However, if you're filing an unreasonable behaviour petition when no one is really 'at fault' (you just don't want to wait two years to divorce), you may want to ask for half of the costs or none at all. Every situation is different so you'll need to consider what seems fair for you and your spouse.

If you're not sure whether your spouse will respond to your divorce petition, it's best to ask for them to pay all your costs. This is because, if they don't reply, you'll have to pay for a court bailiff to give the petition to them in person. Clearly, you'll want them to repay those unnecessary costs (currently £110).

Understanding the 'prayer' at the end of the petition

This section causes so much alarm, and frequently sends people rushing off to a solicitor for advice. But, in practice, the options given in the prayer mean nothing at this stage; they're simply an indication that you might want to apply for these financial remedies later. As explained in Chapter 1, the divorce itself and the financial proceedings are separate. Nothing can happen in the divorce proceedings except the divorce itself. Also, remember that the court never does anything unless you ask it to (usually accompanied by a large fee). These tick boxes are not a request for an order, just an indication of a possible request at a later date.

There are two reasons for putting these options in the divorce petition. The first is that, if you apply to the court for a financial consent order, and I strongly recommend that you do (see Chapter 6), the ticks in these boxes can count as your application and save you having to fill in the 12-page application form, named Form A. As a tree lover, I ask you to please tick all the boxes! The second reason is that, if you were to remarry before you have your financial settlement finalised, you wouldn't be able to get a financial order from the court unless you'd ticked these boxes.

Ultimately, ticking the boxes in the prayer has no effect now, and puts you under no obligation to do anything further at any time in the future. It's like taking an umbrella when you go out: if it doesn't rain, you won't use it. Solicitors always take umbrellas with them, and they always tick all the boxes. So, if you've received a fully ticked divorce petition, there's no need to worry, it's standard procedure and it doesn't prejudice you in any way at all. But it may just help to save a tree.

What to do when you receive a divorce petition

It always hurts to receive a divorce petition. Even if you're at a point where you want to be divorced, it's not what you intended when you married and it can be horrible seeing it all spelled out in black and white. It's therefore vital to understand the procedure here and not let the emotions you're bound to feel cloud your judgement and how you respond.

If you've received a petition based on your adultery or unreasonable behaviour, it's not going to make for happy reading, and you may not agree with all that's been said about you. But all the court is interested in is whether you agree that the marriage has broken down and can't be saved. If you do, it's best to write on the form that you agree that the marriage has broken down but that you dispute one or some of the allegations made against you. (You don't need to say which, and don't dispute them all or there'll be no ground for the divorce!)

Remember, whatever is said about you in the petition has no effect on any other court action in relation to your children or your financial settlement. (Unless extremely serious allegations are made about your behaviour, in which case, you should take some legal advice.)

No one else will see the divorce petition; all court documents (other than orders made by the court) in family proceedings are private and must not be shown to anyone else. The only document anyone else will ever see is the decree absolute, and the grounds for the divorce aren't mentioned on that. Therefore, you have nothing to worry about by saying you admit the allegations and don't intend to defend (oppose) the divorce. The allegations or grounds are there solely for the purpose of proving entitlement to a divorce in our fault-based system. Hopefully, in time, the system will change.

You may feel angry, or wish to defend the divorce for some reason, but there's almost never a good one. If one party has sent a divorce petition to the court, they are clearly saying the marriage has broken down and a judge won't force them to stay in that marriage. It's clearly a case you can't win. Besides, defending the divorce is about more than just saying so on a form; you also then have to prepare, file and serve an answer to the petition. The court fee alone for this is £245 (at the time of writing) and you'll most likely have to pay a solicitor to draft the answer for you. You need to think carefully whether all this expense and time is justified for a case you're definitely going to lose.

You'll also be asked on the acknowledgement of service form whether you object to paying the costs of the divorce. You may need to ask your spouse, or their solicitor if they have one, what the costs will actually amount to before you answer this, because, as well as the court fee, you would have to pay any fees for solicitors or online services that your spouse has used. If you don't want to pay some or all of the fees, it's best to negotiate with your spouse or their solicitor before you return the form to the court. You're in a good bargaining position, as you can say you'll return the form to the court if they agree to limit your costs to half, or a specific amount, or even none at all. You've nothing to lose by asking. You can then write on the form what's been agreed, for example, 'Yes [I object]. The petitioner has agreed not to claim costs' or 'Yes. I agree to pay only half the costs [or costs limited to £X]'.

If you really can't reach an agreement about the costs, you may have to attend a court hearing where a judge will decide for you.

Please note that you can't hold up the divorce for very long by not returning the acknowledgement of service form. If you take longer than 21 days, the petitioner can ask a court bailiff to come to your house or place of work to give you the petition personally. Then, the court will know you've received it and the divorce can proceed. The petitioner will almost certainly ask the court to order you to pay the bailiff fee on top of the other costs of the divorce.

The petitioner is not likely to ask for the bailiff service if you're talking to them, or their solicitor, about the petition (say, if you're negotiating over costs), so it's wise to keep the lines of communication open, if you can.

Applying for the decree nisi

The court sends a copy of the respondent's acknowledgement of service to the petitioner, who is then able to apply for a decree nisi by filling in a couple of simple forms and sending them to the court.

The court then sends both parties a notice telling them the date the decree nisi will be granted. This means it will be read out in open court with a long list of other decree nisis. Anyone can attend open court (whereas all other family proceedings are private), but there's no need for you to attend. The only exception is if there's a dispute about the costs of the divorce, in which case, the court may tell you to attend.

Your decree nisi is a conditional order, which means you're entitled to a divorce, but you are not divorced until the decree absolute has been granted.

Once you have your decree nisi, your agreement for a financial order (consent order, see Chapter 6) can be sent to the court.

Applying for the decree absolute

The petitioner is able to apply for the decree absolute six weeks and one day after the pronouncement of the decree nisi.

However, if you do not have a financial order by this time, it may be prudent to hold off on applying for your decree absolute until you have the financial order sorted.

To apply for a decree absolute, the petitioner just needs to send a simple form to the court. A week or two later, both parties receive copies of the decree absolute from the court. Please note that this document is an unceremonious piece of A4 paper, which some people don't recognise as the evidence that they're finally divorced and legally free to remarry.

A little word of warning if you're about to remarry: don't fix a date for your wedding until you have your decree absolute in your hand. The petitioner is not obliged to send in the request for the decree absolute in any hurry (they have 12 months after the decree nisi in which to apply). If a respondent wants to apply for the decree absolute themselves, they have to wait another three months after the six weeks and one day is up.

Make sure you keep your decree absolute safe. You'll have to produce this if you wish to remarry (and perhaps in other circumstances too, if you have to prove your marital status), and you won't be able to get another copy from the court if they've lost your file (it's not uncommon) or if you've lost your court number.

Making new wills

Although your will itself is still valid after divorce (unlike when you marry), any clause leaving anything to your ex will no longer be valid. It's therefore important to make a new will as soon as you can after reaching your financial settlement and getting your decree absolute.

If you remarry, your will is not valid at all, so, again, it's important to make a new one as soon as possible.

Busting common divorce myths

Let's look at some common myths around the divorce petition and eligibility for divorce.

'We can get a divorce on the basis of our irreconcilable differences'

This is true in America but, unfortunately, at the time of writing, it's not possible in England and Wales. Solicitors are ever hopeful there will be a change in the law but, at the moment, you have to use one of the four grounds explored earlier in the chapter.

'We've been sleeping in separate rooms for over two years, so we can divorce on the basis of two years' separation'

Although you can be separated under the same roof, the two years' separation ground says you have to have lived as if you were in different places. This means you don't eat together, cook or shop for each other, do each other's washing or any of the other things you commonly do together or for each other when living under the same roof.

'I want to marry my new partner but my spouse won't agree to a divorce. So I'll apply for one on the grounds of my adultery'

This ground is only available to the 'faithful' spouse. You can't apply for divorce on the basis of your own adultery. If both parties have committed adultery, then, yes, either party can apply for a divorce – but only on the basis of the other's adultery, not their own.

CHAPTER 8
DEALING WITH
EXTREME SCENARIOS

I've included this chapter because these difficult scenarios have been increasingly occurring amongst my clients, but I sincerely hope that most readers will not need it. There are extreme scenarios where there is a very abusive relationship and one party and probably the children are at risk. A spouse may have mental health issues to varying degrees, some of a temporary and others of a long-term nature.

Bad behaviour when going through a separation or divorce is pretty common due to the extreme emotions which are a normal reaction to what's happening, and it doesn't mean a person has a mental health problem or a personality disorder. Beware of escalating your separation into a war by pinning labels on each other; this could make for an unnecessarily acrimonious divorce with negative consequences for your children. It's usually more helpful to focus on specific behaviour rather than labels, and even more helpful to focus on where you're going and how you're going to get there.

It's not unheard of for some people whose relationships break down to 'diagnose' their partner as having some form of mental disorder, which justifies their own actions or helps them rationalise what's happening. Others will have no idea that there may be anything wrong with their partner, believing all the problems to be down to themselves. The descriptions that follow are intended to help people recognise when they've been in a long-term abusive relationship.

If there's even a possibility that you may find yourself in court due to any difficult scenario, it's important to keep a daily log of any abusive words or behaviour of your ex, and any reactions of your children (behaviour or verbal) to the situation. Date every entry you make as this makes your evidence far more credible. And, of course, make sure you keep any written or digital evidence. If it's a note left on the kitchen table, be sure to add the date to it.

Narcissistic personality disorder (NPD)

As this is more commonly found in men than women 'he' and 'his' have been used throughout this section, but it's certainly true that women can have NPD too.

How do you know if your partner has this? People with NPD will often:

- Be charming, and may be a flirt and have affairs.
- Put themselves on a pedestal, and be conceited, boastful, pompous, arrogant and pretentious.
- Believe they are 'special' and unique and can only be understood by, or should associate with, other special or high-status people (or institutions).
- Be preoccupied with fantasies of unlimited success, power, brilliance, beauty, or ideal love.
- Feel a sense of entitlement to special treatment and obedience from others.
- Exploit others for personal gain.
- Belittle and look down on others.
- Insist on having the best of everything.
- React to criticism with rage or contempt.
- Need constant admiration from others.
- Be intensely jealous of others.
- Be unable or unwilling to recognise the needs and feelings of others.
- Monopolise the conversation and make it about themselves.
- Blame others rather than taking responsibility for problems.
- Express little emotion and rarely show empathy for others.
- Show no awareness of their abusive behaviour or the effect of it on others.

If your partner has serious NPD, you'll always be the one trying to 'fix' the relationship, and will feel as though you're walking on eggshells. Unfortunately, your relationship can't be fixed, and you need to get out the best and fastest way you can, though divorcing such a person isn't easy. You're not going to be forgiven for abandoning him and ruining his life and your divorce is likely to get nasty. If you look at the list above, you'll soon see why mediation isn't going to work, even if he'd agree to go; negotiation is not a word in this man's vocabulary. As retaliation and a big fight will be uppermost in his mind, court proceedings are almost inevitable.

Meanwhile, he'll be making all sorts of outrageous allegations about you to your family and friends, usually under the guise that you need help. However, any expressions of care or concern for you or the children are manipulation; the only person he cares about is himself. You mustn't respond to them, but if you listen carefully to the allegations he makes about you, you'll often realise he's actually talking about himself. (Again.)

You may receive hundreds of messages each day. Half of them will be telling you what a despicable person you are and what he's going to do to you, and the others will say how much he loves you and wants you back. One client of mine was at her wits' end with aggressive litigation issued against her by her husband for custody of their children, and he was trying very hard to prevent her getting a fair financial settlement. But then, on Christmas day, he left an expensive festive hamper on her doorstep!

The only way to deal with your spouse is to refuse to engage in his retaliations and manipulations. Remember, what he craves is your attention. However inflammatory his remarks, reply only to his emails that absolutely require a response, such as what time he's picking up the children. Always limit your replies to the smallest number of business-like words possible. Don't be tempted to argue or be drawn into his dysfunctional diatribes; you can't win and your aim is to get out, not score points.

Be alive to his diversionary tactics and work out his patterns, for example, how does he normally respond when in the wrong? When you're discussing a matter of importance or concern, he's likely to change tack and start accusing you of something totally unrelated. If your pattern in the relationship was to defend yourself, it'll take an effort not to do that. Try to remain focused on the real issues. However hurt you feel by what he's said, as soon as you react, you've lost the battle. Take back your power and act from your head, not your heart.

If you have children, they will usually be his weapon of choice – though that won't preclude him from fighting over your money and property too. His anger may last for years and he'll thrive on constant conflict. He knows that trying to take the children from you for as much time as he can will hurt you the most, and his lack of empathy means he doesn't give a thought for the damage he'll do to his own children. As he probably didn't have a particularly good relationship with them before your separation, and he isn't able to recognise or meet their emotional needs, you'll want to do all you can to limit the time he has with them.

When dealing with lawyers, the court and the Children and Family Court Advisory and Support Service (Cafcass), you'll either be thought of as part of a 'high-conflict couple' that someone just has to make decisions about, or as an over-anxious mother whose concerns about this charismatic father just can't be serious. Unfortunately, emotional abuse is hard to prove and you may not be believed; his charming lies are somehow more convincing than your simple honesty. You don't have his skills for manipulating the legal system and you'll have lost your confidence if you've lived with his abuse for any length of time.

You need to keep a daily log of everything he says, and anything untoward that your children do or say in relation to him, or behaviour that's out of character. Don't reply to his texts or emails, but don't delete them either, as you don't know if or when you might need them as evidence.

Much of the advice in this book won't apply to you if you're divorcing someone with NPD. You'll probably need a solicitor sooner rather than later, but do make sure you take your time and find the right person. Most importantly, your solicitor mustn't have NPD traits themselves and treat you in a similar way to your ex; somehow we often seem to attract more of the same! It's essential that your solicitor has an understanding of abusive relationships and it will certainly help if they have some knowledge and/or experience of dealing with NPD, although you'll find it'll help you more if you focus on the particular behaviour of your spouse rather than the label.

Helen's story

When Ken and I got together, I knew that he had come from a troubled background but he convinced me that he had 'dealt with it'.

I can only describe Ken's treatment of me as like an annihilation of my personality, after which I had to completely reconstruct myself. He put me on a pedestal and then slowly dismantled me. I was so afraid of him but didn't realise how what I was saying was so distorted. He was gas-lighting me, playing mind games to such an extent I didn't trust myself any more. I went from a strong person to someone unable to decide when to put the laundry on for fear of doing the wrong thing and getting the wrong response. With NPDs, the persona outside the front door is totally different to the one behind it.

I had two children by my first marriage and another two with Ken. He didn't make as much effort to get on with my eldest two, who never really took to him. They came to the absolute end of the road with him when he beat up their father. Instead of leaving, I went straight to the police station to pick Ken up. He was prosecuted and I had to go to court as a witness for him. I didn't realise until I left how he thrives on drama, but I thrive on peace.

It took me another six months to be able to leave Ken and my eldest has never really forgiven me for this. I feel really sad that I'm not as close to him as to the other three. At one point, Ken sold my car and used the money to take a trip with one of his children from a previous marriage. I didn't have any fight left in me to protest. It was only when my two eldest children, who were over 16, told me they weren't coming home again while Ken was still there, that I found the courage to tell him our relationship was over.

I was due to go to Scotland with Ken to visit his family, but I went to my family instead. My brother drove me back to my house to collect as many of our belongings as we could fit into his car and, within a couple of hours, my mobile phone had been cut off.

My phone contract was in Ken's name (part of the 'pedestalisation' process, as I'd only had a 'pay as you go' phone until then). I was furious at the time, but quickly realised he'd done me a huge favour as he could no longer contact me, except by email.

Ken's emails to me were dreadful. They vacillated from 'I can't believe this is happening, I love you and need you back' to calling me all the names under the sun two hours later. Reading them wasn't doing me any good, so I got a new email address and my best friend took over and monitored the old account and told me anything I really needed to know from Ken's emails. In one email, sent to both me and my father, Ken said he'd told the police that my father had murdered my mother, and said I'd told him that's what had happened. I was shocked that Ken's fabrications would go to such wild extremes but worse was to come.

Ken applied for residence of our two children, making allegations that I was an unfit mother, took drugs and abused alcohol. In fact, it was he who took drugs and drank to excess and he's certainly an unfit parent, but it's not easy at the time to recognise when an NPD is talking about themselves!

I went to a solicitor but found I didn't get on with her, largely because she seemed to have no understanding of abuse. So I changed to another who was brilliant and who instructed a really good barrister.

Cafcass, an appalling system in my view, made a report for the court but it was done by someone largely unqualified to meet young children, assess their needs and wishes, and fill in the words they don't say. And she, too, had no understanding of abusive behaviour. I made a complaint because the report did not reflect what the children had said. Ken also made a complaint about her – just because that is his modus operandi. In his statements to the court, he made such allegations against me and others (drink, drugs, sexual exploits, etc.) that the judge kept saying 'we can't ignore that'. Every time we got near to a conclusion, Ken would make another allegation to keep the drama going and the game being played.

In the end, rather than fighting on (I'd already spent over £10,000 in legal fees), I agreed to fortnightly contact and to give Ken our address and information about the children's progress. We had, by this time, moved a long distance away from him and I was not too worried by the frequency of the contact, as he had already missed so many visits.

I learned to keep my email contact with Ken to an absolute minimum, replying with the fewest possible words, and only to questions relating to the children. He gradually lost interest until now we don't hear from him at all.

In the early days, I felt a lot of shame about the things I'd done, because I'd fallen for his story. I trained to become a counsellor and the four years of psychotherapy was significant in my healing. I'm now happily single, have a good relationship with all my children, and I've just bought a camper van and am looking forward to travelling alone.

If your spouse suffers from NPD, you won't be able to co-parent or make a parenting plan. Instead, you need to think more about making and keeping your own boundaries and protecting your children as much as you can. You do need your own divorce plan/strategy, and clarity about your aims in your divorce. You may have only one goal: to get out alive.

You can't win, because you're up against someone who's determined to win at all costs. Even if you offered him every last penny, it still wouldn't be enough to make him go away. As Helen's story shows, often the best way forward is to not react to the drama, and to keep your contact to the absolute, child-related essentials only.

Alcohol or other addictions

If you've been living with an alcoholic for a long time, it's clearly been a hard decision for you to leave. This may be because you still love your spouse, because you fear the consequences of leaving, or because you're a kind person who finds it hard to walk out on someone who's sick. Or it may be because you're co-dependent.

Whatever the reason, if you've been trying to help or cure your spouse for all this time, and it's not worked, it's time to go. You don't do a spouse any favours by staying to prop them up, it just enables them to carry on doing what they're doing, and not face the consequences. What message does your staying in this marriage send to your children? And what harm might the children come to by staying in this toxic and perhaps frightening environment? You may feel guilty about leaving your spouse, because guilt is hard-wired into us and we're brought up not to hurt people. However, even in a relationship, we can only ever be responsible for ourselves; you're not responsible for your spouse, or their behaviour.

You, more than anyone, need to make a plan for your divorce, and find someone to help you stick to your plan. Al-Anon could be a good place to find support and to hear from others who've done what you're about to do, and come out the other side. If you can afford counselling, that would also support you and keep you on track. Once you've told your spouse you intend to leave/divorce, you must stick to that, and not just threaten to leave, because, when they drink again and you don't go, you're effectively saying their drinking is okay.

The disease often makes alcoholics deceitful and manipulative, so be sure to collect and keep all the evidence you can. Keep a daily log of events, emails and text messages, and all financial information.

Once you've left, your children may need regular access to their addicted parent, whilst you make sure they're safe, both physically and emotionally. Buried deep under the alcohol fumes, there's still likely to be love between parent and child. It's important not to lose this in case the person recovers. Besides, children also need to know that a troubled parent is okay. Children may sometimes need professional help to process the knowledge that a parent is choosing drink or drugs in preference to them, and to come to terms with troubling images of things they've seen and heard.

Coercive control

Coercive control is a complex and ongoing pattern of behaviour intended to create fear. It's a pattern in the relationship which seeks to take away the victim's freedom and to strip away their sense of self. It usually includes some combination of:

- Isolation from friends and family
- Degradation

- Micromanagement
- Manipulation
- Restrictions
- Stalking
- Physical abuse
- Sexual coercion
- Threats
- Punishment
- Sexual harassment
- Marital rape
- Domestic violence

The abuser is likely to appear charming and normal, even a hero. Meanwhile, you may be treading on eggshells, increasingly acting in anticipation of what the abuser will think, and avoiding any possible conflict.

Coercive control has been a criminal offence since December 2015, and was brought to the nation's attention by The Archers in 2016. As the story of Helen and Rob Titchener showed, the time of separation can be a dangerous one, so it's very important to make sure you prepare much better for leaving than Helen did. Choose someone you trust implicitly not to let your abuser know you're leaving and get them to help you get your children and belongings into a car and to leave with you to a place of safety. Leave a note if you must, but you don't need to tell your abuser you're going over a 'last supper' you've just cooked them!

Fleur was one of a few people who told me they couldn't bear to listen to the Archers during this time because it brought back such painful memories.

Fleur's story
My husband was emotionally abusive and controlling, but in a subtle, almost subliminal way. He was never violent towards me, although he was to others in the last couple of years. His problems stemmed from an addictive personality and a huge chip on his shoulder about

his education and his roots. I was made to feel inferior and I didn't see enough of my family. The long-term messages I received were things like 'you'd be nothing if it weren't for me'. He was charming, though, and to the outside world he was a lovely man. Eventually, people did see through him and saw that there was no substance to his constant bravado and charm.

It took me 10 years to end my marriage, and only after then did I finally see just how much damage had been done. He had hit the self-destruct button and I could no longer protect my children from the fallout. When it finally came to make the decision, it was easy. The journey to get there was tough, though, and, like many women, I just wanted to protect and keep the status quo.

Everything my lawyers and others said to me during my divorce was really limiting: this is the pot, this is what you can earn, etc. But I instinctively felt that my decree absolute and my financial settlement was going to be my starting position and did not allow people to refer to it as the end! Rebuilding your life with a blank sheet is confusing and scary, but the only limitations we have in our minds are those that we put there. My fear of financial insecurity was immense. However, I doubled my predicted income within five years and was able to provide my family with a secure, stable home.

The person who left that marriage was a shell and it took a long time to find myself again but, nine years on, I'm 1000% better off. However, I didn't realise the extent to which the abuse was still holding me back. I recently had a powerful business coaching session in which limiting myself in my abilities came out through and through. The coach took me through a really personal journey and what came out was the influence of my ex's control on me over many years. It was almost like I would imagine an exorcism to be. I felt much better afterwards and ready to take my business to the next level. Prior to this session, I questioned the extent of the coercive control but, since then, I have no doubt how evil it is and that anyone suffering at the hands of someone else in a relationship needs to get out.

The worst thing all these years later is the impact on the children, although they are over 18. My ex turns to them for advice now. They have become the parents and he the child. My biggest guilt is that, because I don't protect him anymore, they feel they have to. But they love him, and he loves them and I've helped over the years to make sure that bond stays. I do regret not having managed my feelings towards him better in front of the children, as they will not discuss him with me now. The knock-on effect is they deal with his problems without my support, and this is a huge burden for them and a concern for me.

I have maintained a very strong boundary between me and my ex over the years and have as little to do with him as possible. This is partly because I'm still angry with him for the way he treated me, and also because I just don't need that kind of person anywhere in my life.

Normally, I don't let him into the house when he comes for the children but, last week, he came to pick up our son, Sam, to take him back to university. Sam came in to say goodbye to me, and I told him to wait while I went to say hello to his father. I received a text from Sam the next day, thanking me and telling me how much that meant to him. Until that point, I had not understood the depth of feelings that were still bubbling under the surface for my son. I am still learning, and I can now see a time that I will make amends with my ex enough for us to be as a family in a room together without an atmosphere.

Parental alienation

This is where a child is poisoned by one parent against their other parent by constantly bad-mouthing and belittling them, and convincing the child that this parent has nothing good to offer them.

This is child abuse.

It's emotional abuse, just as much as plying a child with a toxic substance is physical abuse; in Mexico and Brazil alienating a child from a parent is a criminal offence. Your child may not be old enough to understand the biology yet but, sooner or later, they'll work out that they're half of each of you. And if their other parent is bad, what does that make them?

Below are some of the strategies used by alienating parents, as identified by Amy J.L. Baker and S. Richard Sauber in their book Working With Alienated Children and Families:

- Badmouthing the other parent
- Limiting contact with the other parent

- Interfering with communication between the child and other parent
- Withdrawal of love unless the child stops loving the other parent
- Telling the child their other parent is dangerous
- Forcing the child to choose between parents
- Telling the child their other parent doesn't love them
- Confiding in the child
- Forcing the child to reject their other parent
- Asking the child to spy on the other parent
- Asking the child to keep secrets from the other parent
- Referring to the other parent by their first name
- Withholding important information from the other parent

Whether or not someone is a fantastic parent, it's the natural reaction of their child to love them: it's hard-wired into us. We seem to accept as a given that children need their mothers, but all the research tells us that children also have an aching need for their dads. To try to break the bond with either parent is cruel, and never in the interests of a child who may lose not only one parent but loving grandparents, aunts, uncles, etc. If their parent is really rubbish (and sadly some are), they'll come to that conclusion for themselves in their own time. Brainwashing them before that robs them of their decision-making skills, independent thinking and self-confidence. Their heart and mind tells them one thing, whilst a parent tells them the opposite. They become confused and frightened, loose their self-esteem and will find it difficult to trust themselves in the future.

Our adversarial legal system encourages the taking of sides and division of the parties into two camps, but it's cruel to make a child take sides and to have to exclude themselves from one of those camps. What they need is to be able to move freely between the two homes, and to feel that they belong in each.

A child may feel they owe loyalty to the parent they're living with and have no option but to go along with the maligning of the other parent. It's heartbreaking for an alienated parent to have a child say terribly hurtful things to them, totally ignore them, or refuse to see them at all, but it's the child who will suffer the long-term damage. They may do less well at school and may later develop mental health problems, or abuse drugs or alcohol, and have relationships which re-enact the abusive experience.

When they're old enough to realise what's been done to them, and seek out the alienated parent, these children tend to turn against the parent who alienated them, and often cut off all contact with them. Sadly, that still leaves them with only one parent.

Leonie's story

I was six when my parents divorced. I remember them arguing and fighting a lot as I was scared when my father got cross. He had a vicious temper and became very physical and loud. I remember one incident when they were fighting and it was my bath time. My father threw me into an empty bath while they continued shouting at each other.

I remember we were going on holiday and, as we were getting in the car to go, my mother never came with us. I did not know why. Nothing was explained to us. When my father, brother and I returned home from our holiday, my mother was not there. Apparently, the house was empty, according to my father's many tales of how she left us with nothing, even basic essentials like cutlery, blankets or beds. He would tell us that she did not want us and referred to her with many insulting names, as well as telling us many disparaging tales about her, in the hope of preventing us from wanting to see her.

My paternal grandmother moved in to help my father look after us, but I grew up quickly and became very independent, taking responsibility for my brother, who was younger than me, so as to avoid annoying my father, who had a short fuse, and anything which could result in a hiding. I felt anxious and petrified of my father all the time. I felt unsafe.

My father remarried within two years. My grandmother replaced my mother and we loved each other dearly, so, when she moved out, it really hit me. I missed her more than my mother. I internalised my problems and pretended to be a happy child, masking what was really going on. I also made sure I was a very obedient girl and tried to please where possible. This affected me much later in adult life as I suffered from chronic depression.

My father did not allow contact with my mother or any of her side of the family. He said there was no family on that side and prevented discussions about them. My father destroyed any pictures of my mother and her family and it was in our best interest not to bring her up in any conversations. He was bitter and angry and thought that he would punish them by preventing them from having access to us. My grandparents did try to visit and contact us but my father prevented them from doing so. He also sent back or hid any gifts or correspondence from them, telling us that they never cared or thought about us. I found out otherwise at the age of 19 when I found my mother behind my father's back.

I have abandonment and alienation issues to this day. The other long-term consequence is that my brother and I now have nothing to do with my father and stepmother.

I used to look at myself in the mirror and wonder if I looked like my mother. I would look at people in the street wondering if I may bump into her and if I would recognise her if I did with no idea of what she looked like. I wondered if she remarried and if I had any other siblings.

I have a half-sister from my father's second marriage and, although I was envious of how spoilt she was and how protected she was by her mother from my father, I loved her and she loved me. My father prevented my half-sister and me from communicating when I made contact with my real mother. I was 20, and she was 8; it was hard for both of us.

My father said he kept us apart from my mother for our own good as my mother was more of a career women and a string of degrading words followed. Later in life, my mother confirmed that she thought we would be better off with my father as he was more of a stable figure and she wasn't sure about her future.

I think my parent's divorce was better than them staying together, as growing up in a volatile relationship with both of them being unhappy would have been a horrible environment for children. However, it affected my self-confidence, self-esteem and my progress at school. I think it also brought trauma to me which I did not recognise until much later in life. I think the alienation, depression and anxiety I constantly feel nowadays is one of the *consequences of the divorce and the way we dealt with severed relationships in the years following. I have big trust issues and I find it hard to love and show it.*

On the positive side, I think I have become a stronger, self-reliant, independent person and a survivor.

It's usually the parent the child lives with who turns them against the non-resident parent, though not always. If a child is already affected by the loss of the parent who they no longer live with, they may well be frightened of losing their other parent too. So, the child has little option but to go along with the rejection of their other parent until, eventually, the alienating parent can truthfully say the child doesn't want to see their other parent. It's also likely that, in this scenario, there has been a lot of conflict between the parents and a child can put an end to the constant tug-of-war by rejecting one parent.

If you suspect from what your child says or does that your ex may be trying to alienate you, or if your ex is trying to restrict contact in any way, you need to take action sooner rather than later. Parental alienation is like snake poison and can take hold quickly, with paralysing effect. The longer the alienation goes on, the harder it is to row back from. Unfortunately, our court system is slow and ill-equipped to deal with parental alienation in a hurry. A better solution might be to get your child into therapy – though the chances of the alienating parent agreeing to that are slim. Rather than applying for contact, you could first apply for a specific issue order so the court can order the other parent to allow the therapy. Make sure you find a therapist who understands parental alienation and can really help. Then, when the counselling is underway, you can apply for contact and/or a transfer of your child's residence to you.

Luckily, there is now lots of information available on parental alienation. Read books and online information, and join a forum or organisation so that you can learn from others and feel supported.

When you think your children aren't safe with their other parent

This is a difficult scenario for a parent to cope with. At the time of writing, the thinking in the courts is that it's in a child's best interest to have as much time as possible with each parent, which may mean shared custody, or living with one parent but spending a lot of time with the other. This, of course, is a parent's worst nightmare if they are seriously concerned about their child's safety for so much of the time.

The best outcome is always supervised contact, but this is rarely easy to achieve and local authorities have few resources for it these days. If there are grandparents (or other family members) who can be trusted and who are available to supervise, then this is usually the best arrangement; the children will already be used to them and it will feel like a natural event. Visits at a contact centre, on the other hand, do not feel natural, either to children or parents, but it's better than unsupervised contact if you're genuinely concerned for your child's safety.

When is it right to break a court order?

Of course it's never right to disobey a court order, although contact orders are frequently breached. Rather than asking if something is right or wrong, I prefer to ask 'does it work?' The reality is that, usually, neither party is happy with the contact order that's been imposed on them, and it's always so much better if parents can agree arrangements between themselves, and retain a certain amount of flexibility. Therefore, I'm always far more concerned with whether the child arrangements order works for the child. If it really doesn't, then the correct thing to do is to make an application to the court to vary the order.

If it's an emergency, and you feel it's really not safe to send your child to their other parent, your first priority is to protect your child. For example, if your child has disclosed some form of abuse (in which case, you should seek professional help quickly), or where a parent turns up the worse for alcohol or drugs, or is about to take the child in a car when it's clear they've been drinking, you need to refuse to allow the contact to go ahead. Return the matter to court as soon as you can; there will be a process at the court whereby urgent applications can be made – sometimes without notice to the other parent if that could put you or your child at risk.

If there's a good reason why contact can't go ahead one day, see if you can get your ex's agreement, and, if possible, agree another day for it. If they won't agree, they have the option of taking you back to court for breach of the order. It's unlikely that they'll do this if it's the first time, as it costs a lot of money, time and effort to do this. But it's always best if you put your requests in writing, and make sure you keep the text or email, together with any reply, so that you can show it to the court if necessary.

The court is unlikely to take any action if it's just a one-off breach and you can produce the explanation you gave, but if it continues, the court has various options. The court can order you to pay compensation to your ex to reimburse them for any financial loss they've suffered as a result of contact not going ahead (such as a cancelled holiday). The court can also order someone to do up to 200 hours of unpaid work. If a parent continues to breach an order, they can be sent to prison, but this is done very rarely indeed, and only as a last resort. You would be given plenty of notice that the court is considering this; it doesn't just happen the first time you go back to court.

I've heard people say they don't want to 'break the law' by going against a court order, even when complying with it may be seriously to their own, or their child's, detriment. But disobeying a family court order is not a criminal offence in the same way as a burglary, for instance, is. Burglary is contrary to the Theft Act, and the police are likely to arrest and charge you, and have you punished in a criminal court. The family court is a civil court. If you break an order of that court, it's not the same as breaking a law of the land that applies to everybody; the police will not be involved. It's treated as contempt of court, because the court has made an order against you and you've broken it. Obviously, it's still a very serious matter and it's certainly not something I'd recommend unless there's a very good reason for it. But, if you genuinely believe that complying with the contact order is likely to cause serious harm to your child, you need not be so afraid of breaking the order; protecting your child is more important than a court order.

It's best if you make the application to the court yourself to vary the order, but, if you can't afford the court fee (£155 at the time of writing) and legal fees (if you feel you can't represent yourself), you can wait for your ex to make an application for your breach of the order.

The other sanction that the family court can use if you keep breaking a contact order is to transfer residence of the children to their other parent. For some parents, this would be worse than going to prison but, again, you would be given plenty of notice that the court was considering this. If you were representing yourself at this time, you may choose to have a direct access barrister with you for the next hearing (see Chapter 2).

The contact order is made against you, not your children; you are obliged to make them available for contact. And, when you have older children who refuse to go, it is challenging for the resident parent, who is often blamed for that happening. The question to ask is 'why is the child refusing?' Ideally the parents would try to identify that together, so there's a better chance of addressing it to make the child feel more comfortable. Resident parents will need to differentiate between a serious problem – which will require an application to the court to vary the order – and a child who just doesn't fancy going. Children have to do a lot of things they would rather not: homework, going to bed, turning off the TV or computer, or even visiting an elderly relative. Refusing to go to contact may, at times, fall into that category, and that should not be an excuse for a parent who is unenthusiastic about contact themselves to let the child dictate whether they will or will not go.

Marissa's story
My mother used to force me and my sister to go to our father's for the weekend once a fortnight. Neither of us wanted to go; our father had a new partner, and little time for us. We dreaded these visits, feeling bored and in the way, and craving attention from our father,

which was not forthcoming. We ended up feeling a lot of bitterness towards him, mainly due to him not spending any individual time with us, without his new partner always being there. We told our mother every time that we didn't want to go, but she was adamant and there was no question of us not going. Now, as an adult, I'm grateful for my mother's insistence, recognising that I probably would not now have any relationship with my father, let alone the good one I do have, had it not been for those uncomfortable visits.

Ask your children what they need to make it easier for them to go. If they're bored, what can they take with them for extra entertainment? If they're missing you too much, how can you factor in extra phone calls with them?

The bottom line is, unless you have reason to believe your children may come to serious harm, it's always best for them to have contact with their other parent. Contact with both parents, however awkward, will bring greater benefits in the long term, both for your child's mental health and development, and in their relationships with others.

AFTERWORD

You're divorced, and you've not only survived, you're much stronger and wiser than you were at the start of your journey. Congratulations!

Whether or not you wanted the divorce, what you've done is huge and the occasion, and the transition to a new life, needs to be marked. You may want to celebrate your new freedom and have your friends and family support you as you venture out into a brave new world. And you may want to thank all the people who helped and supported you through your divorce.

Divorce parties are becoming more common, but you don't need to throw a wild party – unless you want to. You might choose to have a 'girls' night in' or to invite all your mates to the pub. It can be a big, upbeat occasion, or a small, intimate gathering. The important thing is that you draw a line in the sand and have witnesses to support you as you cross it to start a new chapter in your life. You now have the freedom to live your life in the way that you want, although this could feel daunting at first. It's also a way to start your new life as you mean to go on: with a lot more fun than you've probably had over the last couple of years.

Hopefully you've been able to take good care of yourself during your divorce, but it's not always possible. Divorce takes a huge toll on your stress levels and health, so now is the time to make very sure that you look after you. You may suddenly find yourself floored by an acute back problem or a bad case of flu, and I've known people become seriously unwell up to two years after a divorce. So eat the best diet you possibly can, take a little time for you each day, even if it's only 10 minutes, and maybe have a massage or some acupuncture to bring your stress levels back to normal. If you're now a single parent, you'll be acutely aware of how dependent on you your children are, so it's vital that you make every effort to stay well.

A happy parent makes for a happy child, so now is the time to set some goals for your new life and to check in with the thoughts that are inhabiting your head these days. Investing in a coach or joining a divorce recovery group will help you make the best of your new life. Hopefully now the divorce is over you'll have more time to be with your children, and you'll be able to be more present when you do spend time with them. Ask them what they'd like to do; having your undivided attention is more important to your children than watching TV or going to a class.

Particularly if you're working full time, every moment with your children is precious, so have fun and make the most of it!

FURTHER RESOURCES

Personal support

I work with individuals and couples in person in Surrey, and by phone, email and Skype with people all over the country. If you would like a free telephone call to explore whether our working together would benefit you, please email **diana@dealingwithdivorce.co.uk** to arrange a convenient time.

Help for parents and children

Voices in the Middle (www.voicesinthemiddle.org.uk)

Online support for children over 10. The site also has a section for parents, featuring young people describing their experiences of their parents splitting up.

Smiley Coach (www.smileyforlife.com)

Smiley TV for children aged 5–11, plus an online group for mothers. Lisa Parkes also provides a fun, safe space in Surrey to help children (aged 7 to teenagers) build confidence, deal constructively with their emotions, and find the magic in their lives.

Parenting After Divorce (www.parentingafterdivorce.co.uk)

Una Archer runs programmes (Co-parenting that Works) for parents, either separately or together, designed to give them ways to deal with any parenting-after-divorce concerns or issues. Programmes are delivered in central London or via Skype.

Only Dads and Only Mums (www.onlydads.org and www.onlymums.org)

Caring organisation supporting parents with full-time custody to those with little or no contact with their children.

Online legal help

The government website (www.gov.uk/divorce) has lots of basic information, as well as the forms you'll need if you want to do your divorce yourself (http://formfinder.hmctsformfinder.justice.gov.uk). **There is more help on the Advice Now website (www.advicenow.org.uk).**

The Citizens Advice Bureau (CAB) has a lot of useful information online (www.citizensadvice.org.uk/family/relationship-problems/ending-a-marriage/). You can also get face-to-face advice from your local CAB, and some will give advice by phone or email.

And last but not least, there is Wikivorce (www.wikivorce.com).

Recommended reading

The Divorce Doctor by Francine Kaye

An indispensable guide to the emotional journey, providing practical help with all your lows and highs, parenting, finances, getting through your divorce and your life after divorce. At the time of writing, only the Kindle version is available, but a new edition will be out shortly.

What about the Children? by Julie Lynn Evans

Essential reading for any parent who wants to limit the impact of separation or divorce on their children. Explains how to talk to children of different ages and demonstrates the many ways children express their emotions under stress, with suggestions on how to make things better. Provides tips on how to really listen and take action when a child tries to communicate difficult feelings. Full of case studies which make it easy to read.

The Guide for Separated Parents: Putting Your Children First by Karen Woodall and Nick Woodall

Another excellent guide for parents. If you can't manage both this and the one above, see which one you feel most drawn to.

Dinosaurs Divorce: A Guide for Changing Families by Laurene Krasny Brown and Marc Brown

Written in 1988 but still the best book for young children.

Codependent No More: How to Stop Controlling Others and Start Caring for Yourself by Melody Beattie

A classic, offering self-help guidance to anyone who's lost themselves in a partner's problems – usually, but not always, addiction.

DIY Divorce and Separation: The Expert Guide to Representing Yourself by a team of Barristers from 1 Garden Court

If you do find yourself in court, and unable to afford to be represented throughout, this guide will be an enormous help.

A Woman's Guide to Divorce by Phyllida Wilson and Maxine Pillinger

A book by two women who went through acrimonious divorces themselves. Written for women who are using solicitors throughout the process, though others will find much to help them too.

This Is Not The Story You Think It Is by Laura Munson

Although this will not be your story, it will inspire you to deal with your pain and challenges in the best way you can. A good, easy bedtime read!

Feel the Fear and Do it Anyway by Susan Jeffers

Divorce is scary, but if you need to do it, this book will help you to feel more confident and decisive.

ACKNOWLEDGEMENTS

A big thank you to the courageous people who have been willing to share their very personal stories and journeys in order that they may be of help to someone else. The names and some details of the storytellers have been changed to protect their confidentiality.

And thank you too to the person who gave me their story before deciding that, in fact, they weren't ready to share it with the world; it's always good for me to be reminded of just how painful divorce is, and how long it can take to recover from an abusive relationship.

It's been a huge pleasure to work with my editor, Claire Ruston (www.wordegg.co.uk), who's improved this book beyond measure with her additions, deletions, and suggestions. She picked up on the phrases where a lay person wouldn't comprehend my legalese and found the words that you'll better understand. All this with patience and exquisite humour. Thank you, Claire!

The designing of the book has been a big learning curve, and Nicola Humphreys (www.nbmhcreative.co.uk) has held my un-creative hand throughout. I'm delighted by the finished book and grateful for all her suggestions and designs.

Grateful thanks to Susannah Walker for the Foreword, the 'legal edit' and her additions to the text, which will be of great value to the reader. Naturally, any errors are my own. Thanks also to Una Archer, psychologist and parenting facilitator, for her valuable comments.

'Merci' to Véro and Jean-Luc for the loan of their house in the South of France to write in for several weeks. Without your generosity I would probably still be on Chapter 3.

Last, but certainly not least, thank you to Peter, my husband and 'rock', for all your support, and hot dinners.

INDEX